God, Consciousness, Quantum Theory and the Urantia Book

Raul Valverde

God, Consciousness, Quantum Theory and the Urantia Book

LAP LAMBERT Academic Publishing

Imprint
Any brand names and product names mentioned in this book are subject to trademark, brand or patent protection and are trademarks or registered trademarks of their respective holders. The use of brand names, product names, common names, trade names, product descriptions etc. even without a particular marking in this work is in no way to be construed to mean that such names may be regarded as unrestricted in respect of trademark and brand protection legislation and could thus be used by anyone.

Cover image: www.ingimage.com

Publisher:
LAP LAMBERT Academic Publishing
is a trademark of
International Book Market Service Ltd., member of OmniScriptum Publishing Group
17 Meldrum Street, Beau Bassin 71504, Mauritius

Printed at: see last page
ISBN: 978-620-0-09575-6

GOD, CONSCIOUSNESS, QUANTUM THEORY AND THE URANTIA BOOK

Raul Valverde PhD

Contents

i

Introduction

This book is a set of articles that were published in the Scientific God Journal and that have the objective to use quantum theory and the Urantia Book to explain the relationship of our consciousness with the Universal mind.

Spiritual scientists make an effort to merge science and religion. As humanity becomes more evolved and is in the search of a paradigm that helps to reconciliate science and religion, spiritual science has the potential to start to spread around the globe and become the new paradigm for the man of the future that does not longer need organized religions but only support and guidance to discover the God within. The book proposes the quantum consciousness paradigm to understand our consciousness and relationship with God. This paradigm explains that our true consciousness does not exist in our brains or in our bodies, but this illusion of our individual bodies along with the misinformation of our true origins has manifested the idea that we all think independently from one another. However, this paradigm explains that there is a common spiritual bond between all things in the universe and that we are all part of a divine intelligence. The quantum consciousness paradigm explains there is no present, future and past but only a constant present. The human kind is always evolving and what was called before religion then becomes science in modern times. The book aims at using the quantum paradigm to explain human mind and body, and their interaction with the spirit, this last one as the main driver of existence for evolution purposes. The Urantia book reveals the nature of human consciousness and supports with its theology the quantum consciousness model paradigm that has been used in recent years to support a multidimensional view of the human mind and modern humanistic and spiritual psychology paradigms such as transpersonal psychology. It also explains that every human is connected to the Universal mind or God through a source of light in a central Universe. This book aims at viewing the Urantia book as key to support the proposed quantum consciousness model paradigm.

.

Article

What is God? A Spiritual Science approach

Raul Valverde[*]

Concordia University, Canada

Abstract

Spiritual scientists make an effort to merge science and religion. As humanity becomes more evolved and is in the search of a paradigm that helps to reconciliate science and religion, spiritual science has the potential to start to spread around the globe and become the new paradigm for the man of the future that does not longer need organized religions but only support and guidance to discover the God within. The discovery of God is a personal matter that requires more than a life time, however, it is the final goal of man to become unified with God. Spiritual science uses concepts from different fields including metaphysics, quantum physics, and parapsychology into a unified system that describes the multi-dimensional nature of man and the universe. The article proposes quantum physics as a possible answer to the scientific explanation of God's living within our consciousness and presents the spiritual science paradigm as a scientific method for the understanding of God.

Keywords: Metaphysics, quantum physics, Scientific GOD, spiritual Science.

1. Introduction

The great question in all the ages has been, "Who, or What, is God?" The answer to that question in all the ages has been determined by the degree of spiritual evolution and intelligence of the people who answer the question. It is an important question.

Who, or What, is God?

In order to understand God, it has been necessary for man to examine his handiwork, his creation. Great progress in the world has been made by a few men and women who have not been satisfied to think the same way everyone else thought about God in their times and decided to discover God although the established paradigms of their times; they have wanted to know the truth about these mighty problems that have claimed their attention. They like to go out on expeditions of their own. They are the Socrates, Plato, Moses, Jesus and Luther. Many people through history have died for their revolutionary view of God that has not been in accordance to the definition of

---

[*] Correspondence: Raul Valverde, Concordia University, Canada. E-mail: raul.valverde@concordia.ca

1

Scientific GOD Journal | October 2018 | Volume 9 | Issue 7 | pp. 503-508
Valverde, R., *What is God? A Spiritual Science approach*

God of their time.

What, is God?" is determined by the mental and spiritual level of evolution of the people and the age in which the question is propounded. Likewise, the answer to that question may satisfy in one age and degree of spiritual evolution, but it will not answer for another age and degree of spiritual evolution. The progress involved in the answer to that question in one age will not be satisfactory progress involved in answering the same question in another age. Man is unfolding and developing not only physically but mentally and spiritually through the years and this changes his understanding of God as he progresses in his evolution.

The second great question is relative to God's will in the universe and God's program for putting that will into effect. Our concept of God's program changes as our concept of God changes. In the search for God and God's will and God's program, people, according to their state of unfoldment or ability, first study the place where they live, then the world in which they live, and possibly on into other worlds. As the result of their investigation, they come to certain conclusions with reference to God and God's program for man. The next thing people do is to try to convert their fellowmen to their idea of God, attempting to force upon others their own idea of the whole matter. When their teachings are not favorably considered, they are disappointed, feeling that those who reject their teachings (their world view) are hopelessly lost, that they are denying God.

The difficulty is that mankind has taken the wrong approach to teach the concept of God. God cannot be known in that way, and the program for the execution of God's will cannot be discovered by such methods. Jesus said, "If any man will do His will, he shall know of the doctrine." John 7:17 What does this mean?

Jesus said according to the Gospel of St Thomas, "If your leaders say to you, 'Look, the (Father's) kingdom is in the sky,' then the birds of the sky will precede you. If they say to you, 'It is in the sea,' then the fish will precede you. Rather, the (Father's) kingdom is within you and it is outside you.

When you know yourselves, then you will be known, and you will understand that you are children of the living Father. But if you do not know yourselves, then you live in poverty, and you are the poverty."

It means that the only place that we can really find God is within. The only way or place that we can discover and comprehend the will of God is within, and the only successful and satisfactory program for the execution of God's will is to be discovered within.

Many religious systems have a rather mythological background, and a careful study of the principal religions will reveal some similarity in the story of their beginnings. The imagination,

2

as well as deep spiritual insight, has played a part in all religious teachings. The appeal has been more to the emotions than to the intellect, although many of the leaders themselves have been people of great understanding and splendid mentality.

On the other hand, science examines phenomena and looks for the cause in every manifestation. It is not concerned with stated belief, but must know the truth of every proposition. It claims to believe nothing that it cannot fully understand; nevertheless, its own findings contradict that claim. The light of scientific research has brought forth many inventions and discoveries, some of which no one can fully explain. Neither do scientists have a clear understanding of where their knowledge comes from. They think it is clear reasoning of the intellect, and so it is in great measure, but if they closely watch their line of thinking they will discover that at a certain point their intellect seems to have reached its limit and could reason no further. Then in a flash they had the answer they sought; it seemed to come out of space. Most scientists would scorn to call it inspiration or intuition and really believe that they reasoned the whole matter through themselves.

In the past there has seemed to be a deep conflict between science and religion over which it was difficult to pass. Science has been able to explain much in religion that was formerly blind belief, and religion can give vitality to cold scientific facts and make them vibrate with life.

Spiritual science uses concepts from different fields including metaphysics, quantum physics, and parapsychology (Steiner 1999) into a unified system that describes the multi-dimensional nature of man and the universe. The article proposes quantum physics as a possible answer to the scientific explanation of God's living within our consciousness and presents the spiritual science paradigm as a scientific method for the understanding of God.

2. Quantum physics, God and Spiritual Science

Quantum physics is perhaps a possible answer to the scientific explanation of God's living within our consciousness. Quantum physics explains that the universe is made of quantum particles that are the cells of the universe and vibrating particles make different forms of energy and matter (Valverde 2016). Quantum physics explains that at the quantum level, particles that come from the same source are entangled regardless of space and time (Hu & Wu 2010). This means that two entangled particles can affect and communicate with each other instantaneously regardless of space between them. The Urantia book that is a revelation that claims to come from celestial beings, explains that souls are created from a source of light from a central universe where the universal mind resides (Urantia 1994). A scientific explanation to the Christian concept that God lives within is us could be explained with quantum entanglement, if our quantum particles are unified with the Universal mind, this Universal consciousness can be connected to us regardless

Scientific GOD Journal | October 2018 | Volume 9 | Issue 7 | pp. 503-508
Valverde, R., *What is God? A Spiritual Science approach*

of space and be able to understand our feelings and emotions through quantum particle vibrations (Valverde 2018). So, the idea that God live within us can be explained with science and the idea that love is vibration can help us to understand that God's love really lives in us. God can really live through us and experience our lives. God is willing to reveal his nature to those that are willing to look within and communicate to him through the divine consciousness.

3. Metaphysics, God and Spiritual Science

Try to delete from your consciousness every thought that God, the Creator, or Universal Mind, is somewhere separate and apart from you. God is within you; look within yourself for guidance, and you will receive abundantly (Pannenber 2001).

Your exercise, faithfully followed, will help you to realize this God principle within and help to harmonize your body, intellect and soul. To develop your own consciousness of the truth, observe your periods of Silence daily. Daily meditation helps to discover and understand God. God is understood by analyzing your daily life and experiences, it is really by living your life at the fullest that you will be able to understand God. Life is the best teacher for God understanding.

In reality we are unified with all of God in us, and to the degree that we are conscious of that unification we can express the divine and demonstrate the power and perfection of the divine in our bodies and in our affairs (Oakes 1990). All there is of the individual - body, mind and spirit - is divine.

A primary step that leads you to a realization of unification with God is to continually square with the statement that God (Universal or Divine Mind) is all there is. To be unified is to be amalgamated, or joined, put together and made as one, and the ideal of the truth student is to come into a realization of his or her unification with God.

The most important thing in your life is self-recognized relationship with Universal Mind, or God. The whole structure of your life is built upon your concept of God and your feeling toward God. The nature and character of the God in whom you believe consciously will be stamped upon your life and affairs.

Much of the teaching in the past was based upon the concept of man's separateness or isolation from God, or the Creator. It was taught that God created people as distinct and separate beings and placed them upon the earth to work out their own salvation, individually. People were to worship and fear a supreme being whose abode was somewhere in space. If people obeyed the divine mandates they would be rewarded, but if they withheld obedience they would be punished.

For people in the West, the Bible was meant to contain all of God's law and was to be man's guide during his sojourn on the earth. But parts of the Bible are incomprehensible to most people, and spiritual leaders and teachers do not agree on the meaning of many passages. As a result, there has been much confusion of thought regarding the whole question of God and religion.

Many people, to maintain their intellectual integrity, have renounced the distant God as has been portrayed and prefer to hold true to their feelings rather than accept what seems to them to be a doubtful proposition. Many of these people are sincere in their questionings and would gladly welcome a belief that would stand the test of logic and reason, for these fellow men, the spiritual science paradigm might be an alternative that would be bring them to the path of unification with the divine.

4. Parapsychology, God and Spiritual Science

Psychic phenomena and parapsychology support the unity of God with man (McConnell, 1983). Perhaps the most known psychic phenomena that has been proven many times is telepathy. Science has many examples of successful telepathic experiments (Schlitz & Radin 2002). If every man is connected to God through its own consciousness, then every man is connected to any other man. Science and intellect helps humanity in the search of the purpose of man on earth by probing that men relate to each other through a common field that is God. Man is connected through God through quantum entanglement and at the same time each person is connected to each other by using the same process (Valverde 2018).

As you proceed on the path toward conscious unity with the Divine within you, you will find your former value concepts changing. Things that formerly took first place in importance will begin to assume their right significance, which may turn out to be no significance at all. As time goes on you will come to realize that nothing really matters but the fact that "the Father and I are one," or it could be said, The Creator and I are one. How are you to accomplish your purpose in gaining consciousness of your unity with all of God in you?

This is an individual proposition. Each person must do it for himself or herself. Teachers may help you and inspiration may come from various sources, but we must each do the work necessary for the attainment of our desired goal. Some have tried to earn this pearl through their devotion to religious work or charity, while others have traveled to foreign lands to convert strangers to a belief or creed. These people will not attain a consciousness of unity with the divine through such methods. If they do attain unity consciousness, they have done it through individual effort and attention to their own thought life, not through overt actions.

4. Conclusion

As the modern man raises his level of consciousness, old paradigms of concepts of God that were accepted in the past are no longer able to respond to the needs of a man that is more conscious of his relationship with God. A new paradigm that merges science and religion is needed in modern times for this to happen, science would need to get more spiritual and religion more scientific to satisfy the need to learn about God and his relationship with man. Spiritual scientists try to merge science and religion and this would start to spread around the globe and will become the new paradigm for the man of the future that does not longer need organized religions but only support and guidance to discover God within. The discovery of God is a personal matter that requires more than a life time, however, it is the final goal of man to become unified with God. When man achieves this, man will stop suffering and will reach his full potential and will be able to use all his God attributes to the fullest including creative mind and other gifts of consciousness including psychic abilities such as telepathy, teleportation, spiritual healing, clairvoyance and telekinesis that are currently dormant in men because his alienation to God. It is only when men realize that they are unified with God and that the God within is all the power they need to live in harmony with the universe that the search for God will stop and men will start a new level of evolution with a supreme level of consciousness.

References

Hu H, Wu M (2010). Current landscape and future direction of theoretical & experimental quantum brain/mind/consciousness research. Journal of Consciousness Exploration & Research. 9;1(8).

McConnell, R. A. (1983). *An introduction to parapsychology in the context of science.* RA McConnell.

Oakes, R. (1990). Union with God: A Theory. *Faith and Philosophy,* 7(2), 165-176.

Pannenberg, W. (2001). Metaphysics and the Idea of God. Wm. B. Eerdmans Publishing.

Schlitz, M., & Radin, D. J. (2002). Telepathy in the ganzfeld: State of the evidence. *W. Jonas e C. Crawford, orgs., Science and Spiritual Healing: A Critical Review of Research on Spiritual Healing," Energy" Medicine and Intentionality.* Londres: Harcourt Health Services.

Steiner, R. (1999). The philosophy of freedom (the philosophy of spiritual activity): The basis for a modern world conception: Some results of introspective observation following the methods of natural science. Rudolf Steiner Press.

The Urantia Book (1994). Uversa Press, Chicago.

Valverde, R. (2016). Possible role of quantum physics in transpersonal & metaphysical psychology. *Journal of Consciousness Exploration & Research,* 7(4), 303-309.

Valverde, R. (2018). Quantum Theory, Consciousness, God & the Theology of the Urantia Book. *Scientific GOD Journal,* 9(6).

Article

Evolution: A Spiritual Science Approach

Raul Valverde[*]

Concordia University, Canada

Abstract

Over the years, many religions have expressed their beliefs of the creation of the world by God, but they have been ridiculed by evolutionist that claim that evolution is responsible of the creation of the world and all the living creatures on it. What evolutionist call evolution is nothing more than God. God is self-existent and an evolving being and as he evolves, all his creation evolves. This is possible because he lives in all the living creatures of the world including us. Death is part of your own evolution and part of God's plan, without death, the world we live in would be static and things would never change. Creationist are ridiculed because they believe that God created the world in seven days, evolutionist would argue that evidence shows that it took millions of years to create the earth and universe but what evolutionist fail to realize, is that time is just an illusion and only exists in our brains and it does not exist in the mind of God. The time it took for the creation of our world was just an instant in the eternity of the Universe. Evolution is the process that God has created for us to reach him, evolution and creationism is part of the same thing, only evolved beings will be able to create. Creationism is nothing more than the goal of evolution, our destiny as human beings is to be co-creators of this universe that we live in, but it is only with our own evolution that we will be able to achieve this.

Keywords: Evolution, consciousness, quantum physics, scientific God, spiritual science.

1. Introduction

Over the years, many religions have expressed their beliefs of the creation of the world by the living father, but they have been ridiculed by evolutionist that claim that evolution is responsible of the creation of the world and all the living creatures on it (Wolf & Mellett 1985).

The reality is that both visions are right. What evolutionist call evolution is nothing more than the living father himself. The living father is self-existent and an evolving being (Valverde 2018a). But as he evolves, all his creation evolves. This is possible because he lives in all the living creatures of the world including us. Mechanical beings such as animals and vegetables that just follow the will of God, they evolve constantly thanks to the living God within them. God

* Correspondence: Raul Valverde, Concordia University, Canada. E-mail: raul.valverde@concordia.ca

keeps perfecting them all the time, so they can live in harmony with the universe. Our own bodies are part of this evolution process, God perfects our body continuously.

However, our own consciousness only evolves because our own willingness to evolve. God has created us as free will individuals that do not have to follow him as other creatures do blindly but only because of our own choice. However, he is always there in our evolution journey to guide us in this process.

Quantum physics is perhaps a possible answer to the scientific explanation of God's living within our consciousness. Quantum physics explains that the universe is made of quantum particles that are the cells of the universe and vibrating particles make different forms of energy and matter (Valverde 2016). Quantum physics explains that at the quantum level, particles that come from the same source are entangled regardless of space and time (Hu & Wu 2010). This means that two entangled particles can affect and communicate with each other instantaneously regardless of space between them. The Urantia book that is a revelation that claims to come from celestial beings, explains that souls are created from a source of light from a central universe where the universal mind resides (Urantia 1994). A scientific explanation to the Christian concept that God lives within is us could be explained with quantum entanglement, if our quantum particles are unified with the Universal mind, this Universal consciousness can be connected to us regardless of space and be able to understand our feelings and emotions through quantum particle vibrations (Valverde 2018a).

Being able to listen to God within us is part of the process of evolution as within this process that we can learn to understand the perfection of the universe and why we need to follow his perfect plan. To understand the wonders of the universe, all we must do is to be able to listen, meditation is the best technique to quiet our minds and be able to let the divine within us to express his wisdom to us that can help us as a guide for our evolution journey.

2. Gospel of Mary

The gospel of Maria Magdalene teaches us that there is no such thing as sin (King 2003). What we know as sin, is nothing more than error of choices that go against the universe perfection and harmony. Illness, suffering, poverty and many of the negative events that happen in our world are nothing more than the manifestation of the errors of our own choices, as the universe is perfect, wrong choices manifest as negative reactions of the universe to signal our consciousness that we are making the wrong decisions. So, in a way, God talks to us through negative manifestations of our wrong doings, so we can make the corrections and evolve as human beings. Integration with God is the goal of man (Valverde 2018b) but this integration must be by conviction that the universal plan of perfection is the only way that we can follow to reach a perfect harmony that leads to eternal happiness of our human consciousness. Man must be convinced that God is perfection, that he is the teacher that can help us to reach our happiness and that if we go against this perfection, we are just attempting to break an existing harmonious universe that immediately retaliates with negative manifestations as the universal law of cause and effect explains (Humphreys 2005).

3. Death, Time and Space, Co-creation of the Universe

Death is part of your own evolution, without death, the world we live in would be static and things would never change. Without death, Tyrants in power would perpetuate themselves for eternity and you would be making the same mistakes all over again all the time. With death, evolution happens, those hungry of power die and let others to evolve the world for the better. Death is a consequence of our lack of perfection, when we reach a high level of perfection, we will stop death.

Creationist are ridiculed because they believe that God created the world in seven days, evolutionist would argue that evidence shows that it took millions of years to create the earth and universe (Lee et al. 2004). What evolutionist fail to realize, is that we are creatures of time and space that are only able to perceive time as a sequence of events in our brains (Valverde 2018c) and we firmly believe that time exists because we perceive it this way with our senses, however, time does not exist in the mind of God. The time it took for the creation of our world was just an instant in the eternity of the Universe. To expand our concept of the realities of the Universe, we need to understand the timeless nature of the reality outside of limited mortal mind, God consciousness is timeless and keeps evolving and modifying the Universe constantly, we are a product of his own power of creation but confined to an evolutionary system that is restricted by the time and space barriers.

In the world of God, there is only constant present. Since the absolute determines the existence of creation, in that same nano-instant, this (the whole creation) has already occurred, in its continuous present. A nano-instant of the absolute corresponds to all eternities in all dimensions. All the infinite and absolute possibilities of being, already occurred in the nano-instant of creation.

The absolute is the universal mind and in its thoughts gives life, creation and reality to absolutely everything that exists, existed, or possibly exists, whether this is measurable, or not, in all its infinite possibilities. As we evolve more in the scale of evolution, time and space will start to vanish and will be part of the eternal reality of the mind of God.

We live an evolving universe, nothing is static, everything changes for the better all the time. We are part of this evolution process, but unlike many of the creations of God that just follow the evolving will of the father, we are responsible for our own evolution. Our father created us as free will creatures with an evolution plan, he wants us to evolve ourselves because he wants us to be part of his reality as self-consciousness individuals that are able to co create with him the universe we live in.

4. Conclusions

Physics has demonstrated that consciousness and matter are connected (Tegmark 2015), our living father as universal consciousness can create matter with his own thoughts. It is our own destiny to be able to create universes also with our minds.   As children of our father, he wants to be able to share and expand the wonders of his creation, but for this to happen, we need to be capable of understanding his creation and its perfection by perfecting ourselves. We are students of the universe in this reality, our ultimate goal is to understand our true nature and evolve as human beings in order to reach high levels of existence. Evolution is the process that God has created for us to reach him, evolution and creationism is part of the same thing, only evolved beings will be able to create. Creationism is nothing more than the ultimate goal of evolution, our destiny as human beings is to be co-creators of this universe that we live in but it is only with our own evolution that we will be able to achieve this.

References

Humphreys, C. (2005). *Karma and Rebirth: The Karmic Law of Cause and Effect*. Routledge.

Hu H, Wu M (2010). Current landscape and future direction of theoretical & experimental quantum brain/mind/consciousness research. *Journal of Consciousness Exploration & Research*. 9;1(8).

King, K. L. (2003). *The gospel of Mary of Magdala: Jesus and the first woman apostle*. Polebridge PressWestar Inst.

Lee Niebauer, C., Christman, S., Reid, S., & Garvey, K. (2004). Interhemispheric interaction and beliefs on our origin: Degree of handedness predicts beliefs in creationism versus evolution. *Laterality: Asymmetries of Body, Brain and Cognition*, 9(4), 433-447.

Tegmark, M. (2015). Consciousness as a state of matter. *Chaos, Solitons & Fractals*, 76, 238-270.

Valverde, R. (2016). Possible role of quantum physics in transpersonal & metaphysical psychology. *Journal of Consciousness Exploration & Research*, 7(4), 303-309.

Valverde, R. (2018a). Quantum Theory, Consciousness, God & the Theology of the Urantia Book. *Scientific GOD Journal*, 9(6).

Valverde, R. (2018b). What is God? A Spiritual Science approach. *Scientific GOD Journal, 9*(7).

Valverde, R. (2018c). Quantum Theory, Consciousness, God & the Theology of the Urantia Book. *Scientific GOD Journal, 9*(6).

Wolf, J., & Mellett, J. S. (1985). The Role of" Nebraska Man" in the Creation-Evolution Debate. *Creation/Evolution, 5*(2), 31-44.

The Urantia Book (1994). *Uversa Press*, Chicago.

Article

Quantum Consciousness & Spirit

Raul Valverde*

Concordia University, Canada

Abstract

What we perceive with our five senses is not reality. Quantum physics has shown that space and time are illusions of perception, therefore, our body cannot really be a reality if they occupy the space. An experiment to the University of Manchester revealed that the shape of the interior of an atom is almost entirely empty space. The question then became how I could possibly make the world around us see us. Our true consciousness does not exist in our brains or in our bodies, but this illusion of our individual bodies along with the misinformation of our true origins has manifested the idea that we all think independently from one another. With this understanding it seems possible to scientifically explain telepathy, clairvoyance, spiritual mediums related to the transfer of information between sources without physical means of communication phenomena. When we understand that there is a common spiritual bond between all things in the universe and that we are all part of a divine intelligence, this simple understanding will fill all the holes in modern religions included reincarnation and predictions about the future and literally every occurrence of paranormal events or anomaly experiences. We are immortal and timeless, once we identify with the eternal reality and consistent with the quantum vision, we will enter the new paradigms of quantum consciousness.

Keywords: Quantum mind, quantum Spirit, quantum physics, scientific God, spiritual science.

1. Introduction

Being aware is to realize everything that happens around you. It is as if in the previous moment you take an action, before acting you ask to yourself: Is it right what I do? And someone who "is not you answers yes or no. This answer is a rating of the act you are going to execute as part of your own will (Hawnser 1997).

Our mind before sending an order for an action to the physical body, makes a study of the elements required to do this: knowledge, physical strength, skill, etc., and it considers the risks, the consequences, the material benefits, potential losses and damages that these actions may bring to

---

* Correspondence: Raul Valverde, Concordia University, Canada. E-mail: raul.valverde@concordia.ca

Scientific GOD Journal | April 2019 | Volume 10| Issue 3 | pp. 167-181
Valverde, R., *Quantum Consciousness & Spirit*

you or third parties (Hawnser 1997).

The spirit of every human being acts contacting his physical being through his or her mind, which acts with consciousness. The physical brain is a computer with its data warehouse. The mind is the result of energy which acts to drive the operation of synchronizing the mental spheres, which are the areas of energy that influence at different levels of consciousness. The energy manifests itself in different ways to transform the same energy into vibration changes and depending on the characteristics of the vibration is the representation of that energy. The perception of the human energy depends on the direction through which one can capture the vibration that it has now (Hawnser 1997).

Most western scientists assume that consciousness is produced in some form by the brain. There is of course evidence for that position. There is evidence of common sense in our daily lives. When a person drinks too much alcohol or suffers a hard hit to the head, that person does not think clearly. We also have more sophisticated tests of the relationship between the brain and consciousness. In fact, all the theories of consciousness during the last century has been supported by psychologists who have been moving toward materialism that characterized the nineteenth-century physics based on Newton's classical mechanics. These have been trying to show that consciousness is only the functioning of the physical brain. This materialistic psychology was supported by John Watson (1916), who wrote that psychology is a purely objective experimental branch of science that needs no consciousness in the same way that science does not need chemistry and physics. It is ironic that while Watson linked psychology to classical physical knowledge of Newtonian physics this to non-materialistic faced overwhelming experimental evidence that the universe is related to quantum physics that could not be made without reference to consciousness.

Consciousness can be defined consciousness as the set of subjective, immediate or remote knowledge that each being has about the world and himself. There are three main schools that explain consciousness: Neuroscientist, Quantum and Skeptic.

2. School Neuroscientist

Obviously, proponents of this school advocate that consciousness arises from an activity neuronal merely more or less complex, and thus resides in the brain. This is the toughest school in their criticism of the others, which sometimes does not hesitate to ridicule because they are considered unscientific and too uncritical. Despite their sharp historical background, this is a real fashion. Its main champion is Francis Crick (Crick & Koch 2003) that has been dedicated the las

Scientific GOD Journal | April 2019 | Volume 10| Issue 3 | pp. 167-181
Valverde, R., *Quantum Consciousness & Spirit*

twenty years to neurology. Its basic principle claims that before treating consciousness as something mysterious and spurious, we must investigate under strictly scientific premises. If we declare the brain as an organ of unknown structure and possibly irrelevant, we never get to study and thus meet its root functions regarding consciousness. Crick and Koch (2003) propose a thorough study of neurons and their interactions that would pinpoint scientific models of consciousness, image of what happened with the transmission of genetic information through DNA. To do this, Crick and Koch have focused their studies on the system visual uptake in humans, since it is the best known and whose mapping neuronal is more clarified. If you could come to establish mechanisms of neurological type of consciousness to see, perhaps it would give rise to continue other more complex as self-awareness. The problem is that if "being conscious of one self" is a phenomenon od only humans, which does not occur in animals as now it seems, the complexity of studies could be practically be an insolvable matter.

M. Edelman (1993), holds that our sense of consciousness arises from what he calls "neural Darwinism" that would not be but maintaining a close fight together of large groups of neurons to configure a representation of the world. However, neither Francis Crick himself has been free of similar criticism, as has been the case Gerald D. Fischbach (2002), a professor at Harvard University and president of the Society Neuroscience, who has made no secret of his view that the proposed Crick's theory regarding an "electrophysiological" explanation of consciousness lacks enough scientific rigor. Tomaso Poggio (Koch et al 1983) from the Massachusetts Institute of Technology, believes Crick's theory is giving undue prominence to the intraneuronal excitations which could explain a visual scene, to the detriment of other capabilities of the brain as its plasticity and ability to change network connections that may be created by this last system state of human consciousness.

Also, within neuroscience school, another researcher, Antonio R. Damasio (1989) of the University of Iowa, disagrees with Crick in the sense that if a comprehensive theory of consciousness should include how to acquire the sense of our selves, it should not only consider the brain, but the whole body. Moreover, he is also convinced of something that otherwise seems obvious: consciousness is also molded along the life of a human being by interactions between him and his physical and social environment, so a model of simply neuronal consciousness is doomed to failure if not considered other social forms of knowledge and theories.

Christof Koch (Koch & Crick 1994), defends the thesis of the neuronal scheme of consciousness

14

based on experiments with animals, mainly with anesthetized cats. These experiments speak of a certain neuronal synchronization in acts of perception and sensitivity but have the huge problem of the place of "assembly". He briefly explains this point referring to the typical Christmas tree decorated with many little bulbs of different colors. In an ambiguous situation observation, such as a landscape, the neurons would be the bulbs going on and off for no apparent order, chaotically. However, when there is a perception, such as vision of a known face, it happens that a group of light bulbs go on in unison (synchronicity) and in a certain specific area (location), it draws attention of the "neuronal group" on the perception received. The problem is that, by one hand, reason is unknown why certain group of neurons coordinate and no others, and on the other hand there seems to be a unique place to decide how to coordinate neurons and even how often they should be.

Other lines of criticism of current neuroscience, even within their own breast, they are those held by Walter J. Freeman and Benjamin Libet that believe that this is nothing but a piece of the puzzle of consciousness and "the current wave of enthusiasm about it is out of place" (Libet, Freeman& Sutherland 2000).

3. Quantum School

The trend to explain consciousness by applying quantum theories has gained popularity in recent years and, although clearly disdained by neuroscientists, more and more researchers direct their steps this way up. Brian D. Josephson (1962) of the University of Cambridge, winner of the 1973 Nobel Prize in Physics for his studies on the quantum effects in superconductors (Josephson effect), proposes a unified field theory, quantum nature, that would explain not only the consciousness and its attributes, but also all the phenomenology observed to date in terms of parapsychological and mystical experiences.

What we can perceive with our five senses is not reality. Quantum physics has shown that space and time are illusions of perception. Our body cannot really be a reality if it does not occupy most of the space it seems to occupy; an experiment made at the University of Manchester revealed the shape of the interior of an atom is almost entirely empty space. The question then became how we could possibly make the world around us see us if this is the case (Russell et al., 1993).

Our true consciousness does not exist in our brains or in our bodies, but this illusion of our individual bodies along with the misinformation of our true origins has manifested the idea that we all think independently from one another. With this understanding, it seems possible to scientifically explain telepathy, clairvoyance, spiritual mediums related to the transfer of

Scientific GOD Journal | April 2019 | Volume 10| Issue 3 | pp. 167-181
Valverde, R., *Quantum Consciousness & Spirit*

information between sources without physical means of communication phenomena. But when we understand that there is a common spiritual bond between all things in the universe and that we are all part of a divine intelligence, this simple understanding fills all the holes in modern religions and predictions about the future and literally every occurrence of events (Russell et al., 1993).

According to quantum physics, the physical world and its reality, it's just a recreation of the observed. We created the body and reality, as we create the experience of our world in its different manifestations dimensional. In its essential state (atomic or cosmic subquantum micro), the body is made of energy and information, not solid matter, this is only a meager level of perception. According to Tornell (2001), this is energy and information arising from the endless fields of energy and information spanning the entire universal creation.

Another character that has stood in defense of a theory quantum of consciousness was the physicist Roger Penrose (1994), famous for its friendly Stephen Hawking differences regarding certain cosmological aspects and a world authority about the theories of relativity and quantum. Penrose (1994) attacks and almost ridicules those who argue that the artificial intelligence of computers can reproduce human attributes, including consciousness.

Penrose, based on the mathematical theorem of Gödel and based on subsequent his elaborations, concludes that no system deterministic, that is, which is based on rules and deductions, they can explain the creative powers of the mind and your judgment. This nullifies the claim of physics classic, computer, neurobiology, etc., to structure themselves into a complex phenomenon of consciousness. Penrose says that only the peculiar characteristics non-deterministic quantum physics could issue an approximate judgment on consciousness, within a theory that involved quantum phenomena, macro physical and conditions of non-locality. At this point perhaps, it would be interesting clarify that local conditions are not known in quantum physics those capabilities that either has a quantum system, communication instant between parts, i.e., without there being time duration between communication of an event from one point to another system.

Albert Einstein called this peculiarity that occurs in the innermost parts of matter, the universe, "that mysterious action at a distance '. If some concepts explained at the time during "Matter and Energy" understand the model proposed by Penrose relates to the concept of Universe "Nonlocal" to quantum levels, in the sense that everything that happens in a corner any of our cosmos is immediately 'felt', "meaning" for any another.

In his last conference Penrose ventures even indicate that probably It is in microtubules, microscopic tubes that form the skeleton of cells, including neurons, where the complicated interactions occur quantum kind that give their "magic" character, "mysterious" from the point of view of science, consciousness.

Hameroff (1994), claims to have found evidence that loss of consciousness by providing anesthesia is due to some inhibition of the flow and movement of electrons within the

Scientific GOD Journal | April 2019 | Volume 10| Issue 3 | pp. 167-181
Valverde, R., *Quantum Consciousness & Spirit*

microtubules. Hameroff argues that certain cellular elements such called microtubules occur quantum-relativistic that "somehow" do emerge consciousness. The major objection to this theory by neuroscientists is that all animals, including elementary, have microtubules in the cells which It seems to imply that they all possess consciousness. Hamenoff argues that such statement would be indefensible, but it is inevitable the observation of "some degree of apparent intelligence" in all animal species. There is still another favorable group to this explanatory theory of consciousness, which is headed by Dr. Ian N. Marshall (Marshall and Zohar 1997) who through empirical testing system claims to have the key to the issue. Marshall and Zohar (1997) showed that conscious thought emerges from quantum effects. Indeed, it has been found that the ability of subjects to carry out work simple while they are connected to an electroencephalogram (EEG).In general, we can say that the weakness of this group of theories lies in the extreme conditions in which the quantum interactions are observable, for example, the effect of local not manifested in conditions close to absolute zero temperature is absolutely clear that they are not exactly those of our brains. However, supporters of the quantum school, as expected, they find answers to these problems and many other objections, in which are indistinguishable from the other schools that obviously do the same to defend their ideas.

4. School Skeptic

We call the skeptical school as the one whose followers hold that science can never interpret and understand consciousness. In general, this would be so because the secret of "being aware" is not based on a simple phenomenological problem, but on the contrary, the great challenge is to explain that part of "the consciousness that is aware of own consciousness". In other words, the great mystery is that we are aware of we have consciousness, and that is irreducible to science.
This way of seeing things has its followers even among members of other schools, as Penrose, Josephson, and in general those researchers outside the disciplines of neuroscience, as physicists, philosophers, etc. Neuroscientists initially despised these eclectic ideas, then try to ridicule, and finally, in the last years, discussed it to the undeniable intellectual stature of many of his followers.

Jerry A. Fodor (1992), philosopher, professor of Rutgers University, doubts, indeed, that no theory based on purely materialistic aspects can never explain why humans have a subjective experience of it, and we also realize it. The question is how you can have any physical system, like our body, as a conscious state.

Another philosopher, professor at Duke University, Dr. Flanagan (1954) says all tests so far carried out empirically (i.e. based on actual experiences under certain control), test nothing concrete since in all cases it was people especially trained to do this or that exercise, which was to be measured. Such training distorts the conscious content of the individual, so nothing can be said about consciousness in such a case. In fact, the Dr. Flanagan argues that it is possible to talk about different types of consciousness, already even neuroscientists have so far been able to confirm that the neuronal system that perceive aromas is different from that responsible for visual perception. Flanagan is an advocate of a broader theory, which he calls "Constructive naturalism '", according to which consciousness would not only be in the man, but also in other animal species and especially primates. The scientifically elucidate these differences you crave task beyond the reach of human beings.

Daniel C. Dennett of Tufts University supports Dr. Flanagan's line, in his book entitled "Consciousness Explained" (Dennet 1993) proposes, according to the latter, that if something can glimpse regarding consciousness is a triple system that integrates the neural data, psychological and those deduced from human subjective experience. This scheme would accommodate some species of higher-level animals. Within the group we might call "skeptic" of this line of thought skeptic, is Colin McGinn, professor of Rutgers University. In his book "The Problem of Consciousness", makes clear his argument that we are not equipped to understand the workings of consciousness, despite its objective naturalness (McGinn 1991). Thus, in the same way that any animal species can not even guess the meaning of a football game, a bet Betting Community, a single lottery ticket, may be the human species will be off limits of certain areas of their existence, including the mind-matter relationship. '

McGinn explains that any theory that gird strictly to physics, biology, etc., can never explain the meaning of the consciousness. In any case, these disciplines can resolve problems regarding the specific brain functions, but none of them can justify such brain functions as these are accompanied by subjective experiences. He also argues that just as science possess experimental concepts as space, time, load, field, etc., the theory of consciousness is to start managing others who themselves, help with its definition and understanding, such as the proposed: "concept of information", as it brings together physical and experiential or subjective aspects.

Koch, C., & Crick, F. (1994) proposed some further ideas regarding the Neuronal Basis of Awareness. Neuroscientists in principle are not satisfied with anything that smacks -of subject-subjectivity, and no longer be right when opposed, on the road undertaken by McGinn, we could reach undesirable prophecy it is self-fulfilling. Indeed, if we accept that science has nothing to say about consciousness and so we should stop investigating ultimately.

5. Quantum Consciousness and Human Spirit

What we perceive with our five senses is not reality. Quantum physics has shown that space and time are illusions of perception. The uncertainty principle Heisenberg (1958) had an enormous impact today since it is mitigated by modern concepts. Scientists, who once had the physics of Newton, led French Laplace to ensure that the universe was deterministic. This happened in the early nineteenth century. Laplace held that since the universe has rigorous laws, and these know the state of the universe, these same laws would predict the future evolution of things. This thought was going a little further, by stating that these laws also exist for behavior human and

Scientific GOD Journal | April 2019 | Volume 10| Issue 3 | pp. 167-181
Valverde, R., *Quantum Consciousness & Spirit*

therefore ruled all future possibilities of man. These ideas had a surprising success that reaches our days, but now the word determinism is replaced by that of "Destiny". "Everything is written" "we can not escape our destiny" "The future is inflexible". This canceled at a stroke the first and most important gift that we received from God and that is none other than freedom: freedom to live or die, freedom to love or hate, freedom to believe something or its opposite, etc. To which determinism answered with a technique of "a posteriori", because once the man action exercised his freedom by choosing something immediately answered: "Part of your destiny, as the universal laws governed at the time of your choice are really elected for you "Human freedom", from this perspective, was reduced a mere illusion.

Strong implications of the discoveries of Planck, Bohr, and many others not quoted in brevity, it was not fully appreciated until 1926, when the great German physicist Werner Heisenberg formulated his famous uncertainty principle. Heisenberg thought, correctly, that to predict the future of a particle was necessary to know the current speed and position and to study the present time particle that only one thing is essential. However, Heisenberg, concluded an unthinkable difficulty, if quanta content in light waves hits the particle, we will see its position, but we cannot deduce its speed. On the contrary, we have no way of detecting the passage of the particle by a point and another separated from the first and measuring its speed does not allow us to know nothing about its position in space at any given time. Heisenberg demonstrated that one cannot know both the position and velocity of a particle in the future.

The implications of the work of Planck and Bohr had not been observed until Heisenberg enunciated his famous uncertainty principle, just as sure now that the implications of this principle have not yet been apprehended today all day, although there is much debate and are the subject of intense controversy. The Heisenberg uncertainty principle is obvious to note that governs for both particles and for the whole universe so is not possible to predict future events, since it is not measurable even the current state of play as necessary.

Heisenberg, with Schrödinger and Dirac formulated the called "mechanical Quantum ", which is to redefine, since it is not possible to know both the speed and position of a particle, the so-called "quantum state" which is a combination of both things at once. This does not lead to a single result that is not predicted for each observation event, but a number of results are given in place calculating possible probabilities each (from the call wave function). A widely used example is the room where we are, for example, quantum mechanics can predict the millions of millions of different situations the room space can occupy for each of the molecules of air that are there, and likely to be met. One of these positions is that all the air in the room could focus on one of the upper corners, and we suffocate from lack of oxygen. This, however, is highly unlikely, but certainly happen in the time elapsed since now and 46 billion years in the future.
Einstein objected to the uncertainty principle since according to his famous phrase: "God does not play dice" meant that he hated the idea of the final decision on which would likely be among trillions of them at any given time was given to chance. However, until today, experimentation

Scientific GOD Journal | April 2019 | Volume 10| Issue 3 | pp. 167-181
Valverde, R., *Quantum Consciousness & Spirit*

supports fully the Heisenberg uncertainty principle.

Another interesting aspect of the theory of quantum mechanics is the confirmation of the wave-particle duality, relative concatenate with the Bohr theory of the atom comes to reinforce it.

One of the most famous and curious thought experiments the recent history of physics, is the Schrödinger's cat (Legget 1984). A cat is penned up in a steel chamber, along with the following device (which must be secured against direct interference by the cat): in a Geiger counter, there is a tiny bit of radioactive substance, so small, that perhaps in the course of the hour one of the atoms decays, but also, with equal probability, perhaps none; if it happens, the counter tube discharges and through a relay releases a hammer that shatters a small flask of hydrocyanic acid. If one has left this entire system to itself for an hour, one would say that the cat still lives if meanwhile no atom has decayed. The psi-function of the entire system would express this by having in it the living and dead cat mixed or smeared out in equal parts.

It is typical of these cases that an indeterminacy originally restricted to the atomic domain becomes transformed into macroscopic indeterminacy, which can then be resolved by direct observation. That prevents us from so naively accepting as valid a "blurred model" for representing reality. It would not embody anything unclear or contradictory. There is a difference between a shaky or out-of-focus photograph and a snapshot of clouds and fog banks. There is a fifty percent chance that each occurred, but some must have consummated that the cat lives or is dead. Quantum physics is not so simple, as it follows from this simple proposition. The so-called Copenhagen Interpretation that argues that there is a superposition of quantum states living / non-living cat, and it is absurd to wonder which of the two situations is the right until a determined observer. This is the called collapse wave function. At that time the cat was alive or dead, but only at that moment, to be an observer, "the universe would have decided ". Of course, the experiment is theoretical because it is not possible to completely isolate a showcase for this purpose.

Now some of the issues raised in this mental exercise if present in the microscopic reality, include the one by the famous physicist David Bohm (Bohm & Hiley 1984), he says the situation is not possible described and that the cat is dead or alive. To solve the problems of indeterminacy, he suggests a complex process of "hidden variables" that would eliminate conceptually. Finally, not worth remembering the Interpretation Many Worlds of Everet III (1983), according to which the universe would unfold in two: one with a dead cat and a live, in which case we would be only one, but also in other without being aware of it. This assumption is highly questionable since imply a doubling of the universe in every quantum process, thereby dramatically increases the complexity at each instant.

Until about 25 years ago, it was believed that the elementary particles of matter were the electrons, protons and neutrons, as constituent core atom. But experiments conducted on those produced collisions of protons with protons, electrons or protons, led to the conclusion that there were even more elementary particles in the matter. Indeed, the physics scientist Gell-Mann (1964) received in that year the Nobel Prize for the discovery of these particles, which he called "quarks". The study initiated by the quarks of Gell-Mann (1964) set the next surprise in quantum physics. Moreover, as good citizens of the quantum world, protons, neutrons, and quarks behave incomprehensible. A proton, for example, is composed of three quarks, two up quarks and one down quark (Generally quarks cannot be linked in varying amounts three).

The resulting color of the sum of the three quarks must be always the "white", i.e. the colors of them are mixed others to be canceled. Another feature is that the mass of the proton is less than the sum of the masses of the three quarks that comprise. Quarks, when bound into protons, neutrons, and other particles, they achieve such stability, for disintegrate and die "by itself" has not yet elapsed time precise since the universe exists for this to occur, and probably will not be in the future. However, when a quark is released in a collision between particles, it does not pass the half-life of a billionth of a second (Gell-Mann 1964). Another important concept in quantum theory is the concept of the spin.

The spin is an essential feature of the particles and atomic sub-particles, and a brief description is to indicate the number of turns that should give those to observe all their properties. The spin is what defines and creates the differences between material particles and virtual (or forces) particles. For each particle there is its antiparticle, as Dirac predicted (Cooper, & Jennings 1986), this is particle with the same mass and opposite charge (including electric charge). For example, the antiparticle of the electron is the positively charged electron, or positron, which is produced naturally in certain types of radioactive decay.

There are four fundamental forces in the universe, of which all others derive. These are the electromagnetic force, the weak nuclear force, strong nuclear force and gravity. Its action is produced, it is believed theoretically, by the exchange of sub particles called respectively: virtual photons, bosons massive, gluons and gravitons. A grand unified theory is one that seeks to explain that these four forces are different manifestations of the same force that is the same force that ruled in the moment of the Big Bang (Georgi 1979).

According to quantum physics, the physical world and its reality, it's just a recreation of the observed. We created the body and reality, as we create the experience of our world in its different manifestations dimensional. In their essential state (atomic or cosmic subquantum micro), the body is made of energy and information, not solid matter, this is only a meager level of perception.

Our true consciousness does not exist in our brains or in our bodies. But this illusion of our individual bodies along with the misinformation of our true origins has manifested the idea that we all think independently from one another. With this misunderstanding it seems possible to

Scientific GOD Journal | April 2019 | Volume 10| Issue 3 | pp. 167-181
Valverde, R., *Quantum Consciousness & Spirit*

scientifically explain telepathy, clairvoyance, spiritual mediums related to the transfer of information between sources without physical means of communication phenomena. But when you understand that there is a common spiritual bond between all things in the universe and that we are all part of a divine intelligence there is unexplained phenomena. This simple understanding fills all the holes in modern religions chipped deja vu incarnation and predictions about the future and literally every occurrence of events or anomaly some experience.

According to Tornell (2001), this energy and information are arising from the endless fields of energy and information spanning the entire universal creation. The mind and body, from the physical to the spiritual and multiple multidimensional manifestations are inseparably one unit that is "I am". This unit "I am", the studio will separate into two streams of experience.

The first experience as a subjective current, (thoughts, concepts, ideas, feelings, emotions, and desires). The current objective, the experience as a physical body, but on a deeper level, the two streams are in a single creative source (essence), and this is from where we really express and have our being. The biochemistry of the body is a product of quantum consciousness, feelings, emotions, thoughts and ideas, create reactions that sustain life in every cell. The perception of something, it seems like something automatic, but this is a learned phenomenon, if you change your perception, you change the experience of you, as this only has reality in your acting ability, be it on a conscious level, subconscious or supra conscious and therefore this world. Impulses of intelligence create your body in new ways every micro quantum moment, equivalent to the total sum of each quantum momentum to change these patterns that changes the being.

Although each person appears as a separate and independent, we are all connected to the patterns of universal intelligence, also called the absolute and merge with local terms like God. Our body is part of a universal body which in turn is part of the universal body. Our minds are part of the universal mind and in turn this is part of the universal mind.

Real-time, eternity exists as continuous present, is quantified eternity, timelessness is cut by us into pieces, or fragments of time we call days, hours, minutes, and seconds. What we call linear time is only a reflection of how we perceive the series of events or changes in our limited perceptual system is wrapped by the poor use of the brain system.

The sequential time is given by the lack of ability to process all data experienced simultaneously, this would make what is called continuous present. Then the series of perceptions data sequences are processed in the brain according to its own processing power.

If you could perceive the changeless being, the time would be perceived and measured as we know, we must learn to change the ability to process data and complexity of the process, to increase the level of consciousness.

Scientific GOD Journal | April 2019 | Volume 10| Issue 3 | pp. 167-181
Valverde, R., *Quantum Consciousness & Spirit*

When looking at the electron microscope, we are looking at our microcosm, there we see how the quantum particles manifest virtually, a symphony and intelligent orchestration at speeds much higher than that of visible light, if we turn to heaven, we will see the immutability of all or macrocosm.

Each inhabits a reality that is beyond all change, as deeper within us without the knowledge of our three-dimensional or physical outer senses. There is a core of being, an energy field that creates immortality like nature, and manifests as the physical body. This core is the being that is, the I am, the essential being or soul, primordial seed, which is contained in an atom called seed. We are seeds of eternity essential at this stage of quantum eternity.

This is the seed based on new paradigms posed by Max Planck, J. Clark Maxwell, Faraday, Heisenberg, Schrodinger, Bohr, Einstein, S. Hawking, among many other pioneers of quantum mechanics.

They understood that the way to see the world in its time, was very wrong, you are more apparent that your limited body, your self and your personality, (the current). The rules of the principle of cause and effect as we know, have gotten us into the volume of a body and the duration of human life. The field of human life is open and unlimited in its deeper quantum level.

Edelman and Tonomi (2000) think that the whole universe is one living organism with full conscious awareness of self. The consciousness of our universe is responsible for the form and purpose that all matter assumes. Carl Jung (1981) found that there is a collective unconscious connected to all humans. This means that all humanity shares a single mind with one another. This is evident in the world through accounts of shared mythology and symbols. This collectivity is a global example of the unconscious mind of the human body in which billions of cells share a similar signal. Human consciousness is an electromagnetic energy field; this could explain many paranormal phenomena such as telepathy and clairvoyance that seem to probe this.

John Lorber (1978) specialized in children with hydrocephalus, or water on the brain is a British neurologist. Children with this condition have an abnormal amount of cerebral spinal fluid accumulation in the cavities inside their brain compressing brain tissue that usually leads to mental retardation seizures, paralysis and blindness and if not treated to death. However, Lorber describes dozens of children and some adults with severe hydrocephalus but live normal lives. Indeed, in a sample of children with their cerebral space filled with ninety-five percent of spinal fluid in their skull leaving virtually no room for any brain tissue, half of them had a higher IQ than one hundred and thirty.

Some of the best evidence that consciousness can function independently of the brain come from near death experiences, profound experiences that some people report when they have been on the threshold of death. The near-death experiences are very short stories of people who have

Scientific GOD Journal | April 2019 | Volume 10| Issue 3 | pp. 167-181
Valverde, R., *Quantum Consciousness & Spirit*

been clinically dead and then are resurrected or revived spontaneously after a brief interval with the memory of what they experienced during that period. According to Greyson (2010), many people with near death experiences reported vivid mental clarity exceptional sensory imagery and a clear memory of the experience and an experience that is more real, then in their daily lives.

Ageless body and mind time, we are immortal and timeless. Once we identify with the eternal reality and consistent with quantum omniverse vision, we will enter the new paradigms of quantum consciousness. Each particle omniverse, turns out to be an energy vibrating in an apparent void immense, (ether), the quantum field is not separate from us, "is us," that's where it all creates stars, galaxies, leptons, quarks, of all creation.

We are creating themselves to each nano-moment, in a huge capacity and creativity. The human body and all the whole cosmos are created and recreated every nano-moment, the body is a flowing body and potentiated by billions of years of intelligent experience. This intelligence is dedicated to monitor each nano-instant, constant change atrophic and entropic, which takes place in each of ourselves, each cell is a terminal miniature connected to the cosmic computer or Omniversal mind we call all or God of all gods.

Morphogenesis is a scientific term to explain this very shaping of tissues organs and entire organisms (Gurwitsch 1915). Consciousness is the creative force of the entire universe. It has been given many names such as God Yahweh Krishna nature the field and divinity (Hick 1982). The entire universe is in fact a single living conscious organism with complete awareness of the self.

Carl Young discovered that there is a collective unconscious connected to all humans (Jung 1936). Meaning that the whole of humanity shares a single mind with one another. This is evident in the world through accounts of shared mythology and symbols. This collectivity is a global example of the unconscious mind of the human body in which trillions of cells share a similar signal. This parasite called our false ego requires a continuous flow of sustenance to survive. Food fuel and any other form of sustenance is energy. Human consciousness is an electromagnetic field of energy. When this potential energy is utilized it then releases kinetic energy which is used to perpetuate the false ego.

Therefore, no matter how many civilizations rise and fall it is our collective consciousness that creates our governing apparatus not individual people. Here we are thousands of years later with technology that can clone D.N.A., vehicles that can break the sound barrier and probe the depths of space and science that can overcome almost any sickness. Yet we still fail to take notice to the importance of thoughts and consciousness.

In this conscious living universe, there are no laws of nature just habits. There is no extra mile to the universe to enforce a law upon it. The illusion of a fixed law of nature is only the result of the being that has no need for the habit to be broken. When habits need to be broken to ensure the survival of the organism we see this event in nature and call it evolution. The collective mind shapes our evolution.

6. Conclusions

Although each person appears as a separate and independent, we are all connected to the patterns of universal intelligence, also called the absolute and in what religions call God. Our body is part of a universal body and our minds are part of the universal mind.

Eternity exists as continuous present, this is quantified eternity, timelessness is cut by us into pieces, or fragments of time we call days, hours, minutes, and seconds. What we call linear time is only a reflection of how we perceive these series of events or changes in our limited perceptual system that is wrapped by the poor use of our brain system. We are immortal and timeless, once we identify with the eternal reality and consistent with the quantum vision, we will enter the new paradigms of quantum consciousness

References

Bohm, D., & Hiley, B. J. (1984). Measurement understood through the quantum potential approach. Foundations of Physics, 14(3), 255-274.

Crick, F., & Koch, C. (2003). A framework for consciousness. Nature neuroscience, 6(2), 119-126.

Cooper, E. D., & Jennings, B. K. (1986). On the role of antiparticles in Dirac phenomenology. Nuclear Physics A, 458(4), 717-724.

Dennett, D. C. (1993). Consciousness explained. Penguin UK.

Edelman, G. M. (1993). Neural Darwinism: selection and reentrant signaling in higher brain function. Neuron, 10(2), 115-125.

Edelman, GM, & Tononi, G. (2000). A Universe of Consciousness: How Matter Becomes Imagination. Basic books.

Everett III, H. (1963). Generalized Lagrange multiplier method for solving problems of optimum allocation of resources. Operations research, 11(3), 399-417.

Fischbach, M. (2002). Rare genetic diseases—new opportunities and challenges through biotechnological progress and scientific knowledge. European Journal of Paediatric Neurology, 6, A71-A75.

Flanagan, J. C. (1954). The critical incident technique. Psychological bulletin, 51(4), 327.

Gell-Mann, M. (1964). A schematic model of baryons and mesons. Physics Letters, 8(3), 214-215.

Georgi, H. (1979). Towards a grand unified theory of flavor. Nuclear Physics B, 156(1), 126-134.

Gurwitsch, A. (1915). On practical vitalism. American Naturalist, 763-770.

Hameroff, S. R. (1994). Quantum coherence in microtubules: A neural basis for emergent consciousness?. Journal of Consciousness Studies, 1(1), 91-118.

Heisenberg, W. (1958). Physics and philosophy: The revolution in modern science.

Hawnser PE (1977). The Answer. Editorial Diana, Mexico.

Josephson, B. D. (1962). Possible new effects in superconductive tunnelling. Physics letters, 1(7), 251-253.

Jung, C. G. (1936). The concept of the collective unconscious. Collected works, 9(1), 42.

Lorber, J. (1978, January). Is Your Brain Really Necessary. In Archives of Disease in Childhood (Vol. 53, No. 10, pp. 834-834). MED ASSOC BRITISH HOUSE, Tavistock Square, London, England WC1H 9JR: BRITISH JOURNAL MED GROUP PUBL.

Koch, C., Poggio, T., & Torre, V. (1983). Nonlinear interactions in a dendritic tree: localization, timing, and role in information processing. Proceedings of the National Academy of Sciences, 80(9), 2799-2802.

Koch, C., & Crick, F. (1994). CT Some Further Ideas Regarding the Neuronal Basis of Awareness. Large-scale neuronal theories of the brain, 93.

Leggett, A. J. (1984). Schrödinger's cat and her laboratory cousins. Contemporary Physics, 25(6), 583-598.

Libet, B., Freeman, A., & Sutherland, K. (2000). The volitional brain: Towards a neuroscience of free will (Vol. 6). Imprint Academic.

Marshall, I. N., & Zohar, D. (1997). Who's Afraid of Schrödinger's Cat?: All the New Science Ideas You Need to Keep Up with the New Thinking (p. 402).

McGinn C (1991) The Problem of Consciousness: Essays Toward a Resolution, Blackwell US.

Penrose, R. (1994). Shadows of the Mind (Vol. 4). Oxford: Oxford University Press.

Russell RJ, Murphy N. and Isham C J (1993). Quantum cosmology and the laws of nature: scientific perspectives on divine action. Vatican Observatory, Italy,

Tornell H. (2001), the quantum man.

Watson, JB (1916). The place of the conditioned reflex in psychology. Psychological Review , 23 (2), 89.

Essay

The Quantum Body, Mind & Spirit of Man

Raul Valverde[*]

Concordia University, Canada

Abstract

The quantum consciousness paradigm explains there is no present, future and past but only a constant present. The quantum mind is responsible for the paradigms being constantly renewed, because the level of consciousness in the human is growing, awakening and evolving. The human kind is always evolving and what was called before religion then becomes science in modern times. Everything is connected in the universe, and we are just part of this great network of connected consciousness that are becoming aware of this great reality. The mind is a product of the manifestation of who we are, uses the analog of computer hardware called brain, (three-dimensional manifestation), to be able to interact in the third dimension. Energy is needed, from universal mind (pre time and space) in order to mold the reality that everyone creates according to desire, decree and intent. This energy and information arise from the infinite fields of energy and information that encompass all universal creation. The biochemistry of the body is a product of quantum consciousness, feelings, emotions, thoughts and ideas, create reactions that sustain life in every cell. Our body is part of a universal body that in turn is part of the omniversal body. Our minds are part of the universal mind and in turn this is part of the omniversal mind. The origin of disease can be explained with the quantum model of man. The body at older age suffers from a transit failure and it does not reach all the cells creating a small chaos, causing confusion in some type of cells that do not get the correct information, those are the ones that become free radicals causing physical disharmony, also called disease. The article aims at using the quantum paradigm to explain human mind and body, and their interaction with the spirit, this last one as the main driver of existence for evolution purposes.

Keywords: Quantum mind, quantum Spirit, quantum physics, scientific God, spiritual science.

1. Introduction

From the moment the universal mind determined the existence of the creation, in that same nano-instant, the whole creation has already occurred, in its continuous present that we can only understand as present, past and future where we are only aware of the present moment (Valverde 2018). However, there is no present, future and past but only a constant present that goes in one direction (Valverde 2018). The past is just energy that already has been dissipated and recorded in

---

[*] Correspondence: Raul Valverde, Concordia University, Canada. E-mail: raul.valverde@concordia.ca

Scientific GOD Journal | April 2019 | Volume 10| Issue 3 | pp. 222-229
Valverde, R., *The quantum Body, Mind & Spirit of Man*

the memory of the universe, the present is the current energy being absorbed by our system and the future is just energy that exist as a set of possibilities but has not yet been manifested in our present reality. A nano-instant of the absolute corresponds to all eternities in all dimensions. All the infinite and absolute possibilities of all beings have already occurred in the nano-instant of creation.

The absolute is the universal mind that in its thoughts gives life, creation and reality to absolutely everything that exists, existed, or possibly exists, whether this is measurable, or not, in all its infinite possibilities. The paradigms are being constantly renewed, because the level of consciousness in the human, they are growing, awakening and evolving exponentially in the ascending elliptic curve, which the absolute has determined for such events. The human kind is always evolving and what was called before religion then becomes science in modern times.

Thomas Khun (2011), in his change of paradigms, referred to the way in which current science perceives religion and how reality responds to that perception, be these realities formed in the fractal minds from the universe to the personal micro universes. A change of paradigms is then a change in the way we perceive our own reality, and this causes a change itself as part of the continuous system of the absolute (Valverde 2016). We receive by fractal inheritance, in our own body to what is analog to a computer operating system, a replica copy of the universal whole, which allows us to be in a network with everything in the absolute and in everything, from the first dimension to the infinite afterwards, both in sequences and in parallel universes as described by Tegmark (2003), since everything has always existed, through the work and grace of desire, of the decree and the attempt of the absolute. Everything is connected in the universe, and we are just part of this great network of connected consciousness that are becoming aware of this great reality.

The mind as a product of the manifestation of who we are, uses the analog of computer hardware called brain, (three-dimensional manifestation), to be able to interact in this plane of existence, called the third dimension, using the thoughts as elements of process to be able to evaluate the unique reality, indivisible of one's personality (Valverde 2016).

2. Quantum mind, body and spirit

The union of the hardware, (brain) and the computer operating system, (our own spirit), is as a set of experiences and knowledge that is the product of the course of the series of events through which we have spent as much as humanity as individuality, together with the primal energy that supports us, and the sustaining energy of the universe in its fractals, allows manifestation to be in all planes of consciousness. This produces what, and who are we.

Then energy is needed, from universal mind (pre time and space) in order to mold the reality that each individual creates according to desire, decree and intent. From the absolute to the quantum particles in their center of light that is the source of all reality (Valverde 2018).

Reality is a function of the perception of it, and this is part of the conscious momentum. It is known as social conditioning, induced function in which we all end up agreeing to participate, and that must be added the inheritance of our ancestors and all the genetics included in the coding of DNA (programming attached to our own operating system).

The physical world reality is only a recreation of the observed (Valverde 2018). We create the body and our reality, as we create the experience of our world in its different dimensional manifestations. In its essential state, (atomic, or sub cosmic microcosmic), the body is formed of energy and information, and not solid matter, this is only a rickety level of perception (Hu & Wu 2010).

This energy and information arise from the infinite fields of energy and information that encompass all universal creation (pre-space and time) (Valverde 2018). The mind and its bodies, from the physical to the spiritual and its multiple multidimensional manifestations, are inseparably one that is the unit .... "I am".

This unit "I am", can be separated it in two streams of experience. We experience it first as a subjective matter without thoughts, concepts, ideas, feelings, emotions, and desires. Then we experience it with objective matter, we experience it as a physical body, but nevertheless on a deeper level, the two currents are in a single creative source, (essence), and it is from this, where we manifest and have our being.

The biochemistry of the body is a product of quantum consciousness, feelings, emotions, thoughts and ideas, create reactions that sustain life in every cell (Valverde 2018). The material things of the world are shadowy reflections of invisible but more substantial spiritual realities (Urantia 1994). The perception of something, seems like something automatic, but this is a learned phenomenon, if you change your perception, you change the experience of you, since it only has reality in your capacity of interpretation, be it at the conscious, subconscious or supraconscious level and therefore of this world (Valverde 2016). Transpersonal Psychology has used these concepts to help people to transform themselves by changing the way they perceive things (Valverde 2016).

There are impulses of intelligence that create your bodies in new ways every quantum micro-instant. What you are equals the total sum of each quantum impulse, by changing these schemes you change. Although each person seems as separate and independent, we are all connected to the patterns of the universal intelligence, or also called the absolute or in local terms known as God (Valverde 2018).

Scientific GOD Journal | April 2019 | Volume 10| Issue 3 | pp. 222-229
Valverde, R., *The quantum Body, Mind & Spirit of Man*

Our body is part of a universal body that in turn is part of the omniversal body. Our minds are part of the universal mind and in turn this is part of the omniversal mind. The real time exists only as the eternity of the continuous present, it is the quantified eternity, it is the timelessness cut by us into pieces, or fragments of time that we call days, hours, minutes, and seconds (Valverde 2018). What we call linear time is only a reflection of our way of perceiving the series of events, or changes in which our limited perceptual system is wrapped by the deficient use of the brain - neuro - spinal system. The sequential time is given by the lack of capacity to process all the data experienced simultaneously, which would give course to what is called continuous present (Polisena 2017).

Then the data series of the sequences of the perceptions are processed in the brain according to their own processing capacity. If you could perceive the immutable being, time would stop being perceived and measured as we know it, we would have to learn to change the ability to process data and its complexity of the process, in order to increase the level of consciousness.

When looking at the electron, we are looking at our microcosm, there we see how the particles quantum manifests in a symphony and intelligent orchestration at speeds far superior to that of visible light, if we turn to the sky, we will see the immutability of the whole, or macrocosm. There is a core of being, an energetic field of immortality that creates the self as essence, and also manifests as the physical body. This nucleus is the being that is, the I am, the essential being or spirit, primeval seed, which is contained in an atom called seed. We are seeds of essential eternity in this scenario of quantum eternity (Valverde 2018).

This is the base seed of the new paradigms proposed by Max Planck, Maxwell, Faraday, Heisenberg, Schrodinger, Bohr and Einstein among many other pioneers of quantum physics. They understood that the way of seeing the world in their time, was very false, you are more than your limited apparent body, yourself and your personality.

The rules of the principle of cause and effect as we know them, have gotten us into the volume of a body and the duration of human life. In reality, the field of human life is open and unlimited in its deepest quantum plane.

The body lacks age and the mind of time, we are immortal and timeless. Once we identify with that eternal and congruent reality, with the vision quantum of the omniverse, we will enter the new paradigms of quantum consciousness (Valverde 2018), this will expand in its omniversal, radial, exponential and dimensional fractals.

We will be consciously modifying the internal program, based on our own operating system (spirit) each particle of the omniverse, turns out to be a ghostly bundle of energy that vibrates in an immense apparent emptiness, the quantum field is not separated from us, ... "it is us", that is where the universal mind creates stars, galaxies, leptons, quarks, among all creation. Just as Jesus said, the kingdom of God is within you (Luke 17:20-21).

The human body and the entire cosmos are created and recreated every nano-instant, the body is a flowing organism and potentiated by billions of years of intelligent experience. This intelligence is dedicated to supervising every nano-instant, the constant anthropic and entropic change that takes place in each one of us (Valverde 2018).

Each cell is a miniature terminal connected to the cosmic computer or omniverse mind that we call God. The cells of a baby are new biochemical formations, but the atoms that make them up are not they have been circulating around the universe since the beginning of time, for thousands of millions of earth years. The baby is new at the mercy of the invisible intelligence (spirit), which has joined that atom seed and its operating system to give life and unique form of human life.

Every second in each of the baby 's cells, trillions of reactions are all controlled by that unique intelligence called essence or spirit that has its own program and operating system. Quantum mechanics tells us that there are no endings for the cosmic dance, the field of energy and information of the omniversal primal intelligence that never stops manifesting itself, or transforming itself, becoming something new at each nano-instant.

Our multidimensional body obeys that same creative impulse to maintain life. The body must be kept in constant change, the skin is renewed cellularly once a month, the liver every six weeks, the skeleton every three years, at the end of every three years most of the body has been renewed (except the atom seed or soul) (Chopra, 2003). The atoms of the body are no longer the same, they have been renewed, but the human being remains the same, this indicates that it is the holographic field that unfolds the seed atom that forces each atom of the body to fulfill its function to configure a specific body. Only physical death when the gravitational holographic field ceases is when the atoms of the body are dispersed, and cell disintegration occurs.

3. Quantum physics, diseace in men and perception of reality

The origin of disease can be explained with the quantum model of man. The body from the age of about thirty, the information that comes from the seed atom suffers from a transit failure and it does not reach all the cells creating a small chaos, causing confusion in some type of cells that do not get the correct information, those are the ones that become free radicals causing physical disharmony also called disease. This seems to be part of the design of the men's body, but it might be able to be changed with the consciousness of man (Chopra 2015).

Formal science has advanced to the point that the ancient knowledge of our mystical masters, can already check. The spiritual teachings finally have explanation, without ceasing to be the wonderful thing that has always been considered. Schure (1989), the philosopher once said, "the day will come when science, technology, religion and spirituality will shake hands, and realize that

Scientific GOD Journal | April 2019 | Volume 10| Issue 3 | pp. 222-229
Valverde, R., *The quantum Body, Mind & Spirit of Man*

they are the same".

There is no world independent of the observer (Valverde 2016), Everything is an illusion, everything is relative, and it is according to the perception that everyone has of things, it is false to say that there is an independent world.

The world is a reflection of the sensory and conceptual apparatus of the neuro-spinal brain system that registers it. Our dormant system only interprets one part per billion. of what vibrates in the quantum universe. A bat perceives the world through ultrasound, the snake perceives its reality by heat frequencies in the octave of the infrared, bees perceive it in ultraviolet light frequencies.

Outside there is only data and intelligent information, waiting to be interpreted by the perceiver. We take from the quantum soup, the energy flow with radically ambiguous information, and we receive it and through the sensory apparatuses, we select it to be interpreted by the neuro-spinal brain system, creating the own reality, according to the capacity and programming that let's have and arrange for it.

We form figures and geometric shapes in our mind using the magnetic fields programmed by the laws of geometry, to turn it into a three-dimensional solid. Incredibly, one can change the world, including the body, if one can change the perception. Perhaps this last can be the key to cure disease in men.

At this moment, our consciousness is dedicated to creating the body, from the operating system without conscious awareness of one, what we call autonomous or limbic system. This is designed to handle the functions that have escaped the limited consciousness with which we form our concrete reality. In the realities of the new paradigms we can recognize that the material we call solid of our three-dimensional physical bodies are mere illusion.

This field of physicality we call solid, is composed of organs, which are composed of tissues and these in turn from cells that are formed by molecules and these of atoms, which in turn are formed by protons and electrons, which are formed by quarks or quantum particles or quantum.

Mechanics and quantum physics assert that atoms are almost empty space, the particles that make up matter act by an order because information and receive energy to travel at speeds light that quantum space, which leads us to understand that what we believe is solid matter is only energy executing a job, due to intelligent programming that determines and defines them (Valverde 2016).

Thus, a group of vibrations, with order and sense in a certain frequency, rhythm and tone can be encoded as atoms. Each atom has its abstract codes that vibrate in the great quantum soup and to which they respond. The space called empty is printed with intelligent information that even before manifesting it already contains it in a dormant state of being in a myriad of possibilities and

32

Scientific GOD Journal | April 2019 | Volume 10| Issue 3 | pp. 222-229
Valverde, R., *The quantum Body, Mind & Spirit of Man*

alternatives. This is the quantum space that forms when called human and all the matter that contains it.

Just as in brain memory, there are millions of words, ideas, concepts and thoughts, without which we manifest them, in the quantum field of the universe, all the information contained in an unexpressed way in a state of potentiality, but already existing in the reality of absolute.

Therefore, the essential matter of the universe as the own body, is no matter, no thinking, intelligent matter in different states of dimensional conscious manifestation ...

Our realities change as we allow ourselves more freedom of thought, of feeling, of emotions of opening the mind to allow us the possibility that our senses and mind show us an unlimited universe, with its infinite possibilities of being and being.

Edelman and Tonomi (2000) think that the whole universe is one living organism with full conscious awareness of self. The consciousness of our universe is responsible for the form and purpose that all matter assumes. Carl Jung (1981) found that there is a collective unconscious connected to all humans. This means that all humanity shares a single mind with one another. This is evident in the world through accounts of shared mythology and symbols. This collectivity is a global example of the unconscious mind of the human body in which billions of cells share a similar signal. Human consciousness is an electromagnetic energy field; this could explain many paranormal phenomena such as telepathy and clairvoyance that seem to probe this.

3. Conclusions

The paradigms are being constantly renewed as we develop our quantum consciousness. The human kind is always evolving and what was called before religion then becomes science in modern times. The mind uses the analog of computer hardware called brain to be able to interact in this plane of existence, the union of the hardware, (brain) and the computer operating system, (our own spirit), is as a set of experiences and knowledge that are timeless and represent who we are. Reality is nothing more than molded energy coming from the Universal mind and manifested according to our intentions and desires. The biochemistry of the body is a product of quantum consciousness and shadowy reflections of invisible but more substantial spiritual realities. Although each person seems as separate and independent, we are all connected to the Universal mind and possess a quantum system that is immortal and timeless.

References

Chopra, D. (2003). Ageless body, timeless mind: A practical alternative to growing old. Random House.

Chopra, D. (2015). Quantum healing: Exploring the frontiers of mind/body medicine. Bantam.

Edelman, GM & Tononi G (2000). A Universe of Consciousness: How Matter Becomes Imagination. Basic books.

Halliwell, J. J., & Thorwart, J. (2002). Life in an energy eigenstate: decoherent histories analysis of a model timeless universe. *Physical Review D*, *65*(10), 104009.

Hu H, Wu M (2010). Current landscape and future direction of theoretical & experimental quantum brain/mind/consciousness research. Journal of Consciousness Exploration & Research. 9;1(8).

Jung CG. The archetypes and the collective unconscious (No.20). Princeton University Press, New York, 1981.

Kuhn, S. T. (2011). *La estructura de las revoluciones científicas*. Fondo de cultura económica.

Polisena, V. Y. (2017). 6. God plays with a quantum die infinite interactions from the arche. *SOCRATES: VOL. 4 NO. 4 (2016) Issue-December*, *4*, 65.

Schuré, E. (1989). *The Great Initiates: A Study of the Secret History of Religions*. SteinerBooks.

Tegmark, M. (2003). Parallel universes. *Scientific American*, *288*(5), 40-51.

The Urantia Book (1994). Uversa Press, Chicago.

Valverde, R. (2016). Possible role of quantum physics in transpersonal & metaphysical psychology. *Journal of Consciousness Exploration & Research*, *7*(4), 303-309.

Valverde, R. (2018). Quantum Theory, Consciousness, God & the Theology of the Urantia Book. *Scientific GOD Journal*, *9*(6).

Scientific GOD Journal | August 2018 | Volume 9 | Issue 6 | pp. 445-466
Valverde, R., *Quantum Theory, Consciousness, God & the Theology of the Urantia Book*

Perspective

Quantum Theory, Consciousness, God & the Theology of the Urantia Book

Raul Valverde[*]

Concordia University, Canada

Abstract

The Urantia book reveals the nature of human consciousness and supports with its theology the quantum consciousness model paradigm that has been used in recent years to support a multidimensional view of the human mind and modern humanistic and spiritual psychology paradigms such as transpersonal psychology. It also explains that every human is connected to the Universal mind or God through a source of light in a central Universe. The article proposes a quantum consciousness model that explains that our consciousness is immortal and non local. The model also proposes that our perceived reality is created by our consciousness by interpreting vibrating energy. The Urantia book aims to unite religion, science and philosophy. This article aims at viewing the Urantia book as key to support the proposed quantum consciousness model paradigm and the Christian belief that a fraction of God resides in us and connects us to his infinite source of light.

Keywords: Quantum consciousness, quantum physics, Scientific GOD, neurotheology, Urantia book.

1. Introduction

The trend to explain consciousness by applying quantum theories has gained popularity in recent years and, although clearly disdained by neuroscientists, more and more researchers direct their steps this way up. Brian D. Josephson (1962) of the University of Cambridge, winner of the 1973 Nobel Prize in Physics for his studies on the quantum effects in superconductors (Josephson effect), proposes a unified field theory of quantum nature that would explain not only consciousness and its attributes, but also all the phenomenology observed to date in terms of parapsychological, metaphysical and mystical experiences (Valverde 2015b).

The Urantia book aims to unite religion, science and philosophy. The book supports the idea of a unified quantum field and explains the nature of reality by using quantum principles.

In this article, a literature review that supports that quantum nature of consciousness and its connection to the Universal mind is presented followed by a set of experiments that support the quantum consciousness paradigm. A quantum consciousness model with seven principles is

---

[*] Correspondence: Raul Valverde, Concordia University, Canada. E-mail: raul.valverde@concordia.ca

proposed and a table with Urantia book's references that support these statements is presented with explanations on how these references support the model.

2. Literature Review

Hu & Wu (2010) as part of their explanation of the quantum consciousness model, come to the conclusion that materialistic theories for the explanation of consciousness are likely invalid and that quantum effects play important roles in consciousness. Another character that has stood in defense of a quantum theory of consciousness was the physicist Roger Penrose (1994). Penrose (1994) attacks and almost ridicules those who argue that the artificial intelligence of computers can reproduce human attributes, including consciousness. Penrose, based on the mathematical theorem of Gödel and based on subsequent his elaborations, concludes that no system that is deterministic, that is, which is based on rules and deductions, can explain the creative powers of the mind and its judgment. This nullifies the claim of classic physics, computer, neurobiology, etc., that structure themselves into a complex phenomenon of consciousness. Penrose says that only the peculiar characteristics of non-deterministic quantum physics could issue an approximate judgment on consciousness, within a theory that involves quantum phenomena, macro physical and conditions of non-locality. At this point, perhaps it would be interesting to clarify that local conditions are not known in quantum physics, those capabilities that either have a quantum system, experience instant communication between two parts without there being time duration between communication of an event from one point to another system.

There is still another favorable group to this explanatory theory of consciousness, which is headed by Dr. Ian N. Marshall (Marshall & Zohar 1997) who through empirical testing system claims to have the key to the issue. Marshall and Zohar (1997) showed that conscious thought emerges from quantum effects. Quantum physics helped to have a quantum understanding of consciousness. What we are able to perceive with our five senses is not reality. Quantum physics has shown that space and time are illusions of perception. Our body cannot really be a reality if it does not occupy most of the space it seems to occupy; an experiment made at the University of Manchester revealed the shape of the interior of an atom is almost entirely empty space. The question then became how we could possibly make the world around us see us if this is the case (Russell et al., 1993).

The quantum consciousness model suggests that consciousness lives in the quantum domain outside time-space. Fred Wolf (1984) states that there has never been an adequate definition, a clear metaphor, or even a good physical picture of what time is, in quantum mechanics, time is not an observable phenomenon; it is only an extraneous ordering parameter. Davies (1988) indicates that time exists merely as a parameter for gauging the interval between events. Griffin(1986) states that the notion that physics is in some fundamental sense 'timeless' has been widely accepted. Wolf (1984) states that In quantum mechanics, space is an observable. To observe space, we need the observer and the observed. Their separation is 'space.'

Hu & Wu (2013) based on their theoretical and experimental studies have shown that: (1) human consciousness is non-spatial and non-temporal and not in the brain but in prespacetime; (2) brain is an interface between human consciousness and the external world; Hu & Wu (2010) elaborate that the quantum consciousness model includes that quantum effects play important roles in brain and in consciousness such as in wave function collapse. They also explain that consciousness is likely outside spacetime and is the foundation of reality and that conscious intentions likely have physical effects on matter.

The quantum consciousness model proposes that our true consciousness does not exist in our brains or in our bodies, but this illusion of our individual bodies along with the misinformation of our true origins has manifested the idea that we all think independently from one another. With this understanding, it seems possible to scientifically explain telepathy, clairvoyance, spiritual mediums related to the transfer of information between sources without physical means of communication phenomena. When we understand that there is a common spiritual bond between all things in the universe and that we are all part of a divine intelligence, this simple understanding will fill all the holes in modern religions and predictions about the future and literally every occurrence of events (Russell et al., 1993). Unity of Mind is likely achieved through quantum entanglement beyond the current forms of quantum mechanics (Hu & Wu 2010). The quantum consciousness paradigm through the principle of entanglement also proposes that although each person appears as a separate and independent, in reality we are all connected to the patterns of universal intelligence also called the absolute. Our body is part of a universal body, our minds are part of the universal mind and in turn all of these are part of the universe (Valverde 2016).

According to quantum physics, the physical world and its reality, it's just a recreation of the observed. Consciousness likely play important roles in quantum effects such as in wave function collapse that is responsible for the creation of our reality (Hu & Wu 2010). We created the body and reality, as we create the experience of our world in its different manifestations dimensional. In its essential state (atomic or cosmic subquantum micro), the body is made of energy and information, not solid matter, this is only a meager level of perception, this is energy and information arising from the endless fields of energy and information spanning the entire universal creation (Valverde 2015a).

The quantum consciousness model also teaches that our true consciousness lives in a constant present and it is not bound by time past and future. Consider the distinction of past, present and future, what we are conscious of as now is already past, even if only by a fraction of a second. The conscious content of the moment is therefore of that which is past and gone. The future is not yet. The present is but it cannot be specified in words or thoughts, without it slipping into the past. When a future moment comes a similar situation will prevail. Therefore from the past of the present we may be able to predict, at most, the past of the future. The actual immediate present is always the unknown.

Wolf (1984) writes that "The closest we come to observing time is observing what Buddhists call 'being-time.' Everything that is, is, was and will be. Every moment remains motionless and frozen. Past, present and future represent a map for the perusal of the all-seeing being-time.". David Bohm writes that atomic structure dissolves into electrons, protons, neutrons, quarks, subquarks, etc., and eventually into dynamically changing forms in an all-pervasive and universal set of fields. When these fields are treated quantum-mechanically, we find that even in what is called a vacuum there are `zero-point' fluctuations, giving `empty space' an energy that is immensely beyond that contained in what is recognized as matter. In the vacuum state the `state function' (which represents the whole of space and time) oscillates uniformly at a frequency so high that it is utterly beyond any known physical interpretation. Further, "we would be justified in saying that the vacuum state is, in a certain sense, `timeless' or `beyond time,' at least as time is now known, measured and experienced."

With this in mind, it is less than surprising that science is confused about what occurs at the quantum level. For example, L. Beynam, in a paper called "The Emergent Paradigm in Science" that appeared in Revision in 1978, gave a formulation of the well-known Bell's Theorem. Basic principles of quantum theory spatially separated parts of reality cannot be independent, he goes on to say that this "opens up avenues of scientific development for which the classical constructs of space and time prove almost totally useless and meaningless".

Paul Davies (1988) in God and the New Physics reports on a 1982 experiment by Aspect, Dalibard, and Roger at the Institute of Theoretical and Applied Optics in Paris. From this experiment, this conclusion is drawn:

> Either objective reality does not exist and it is meaningless for us to speak of things or objects as having any reality above and beyond the mind of an observer or faster-than-light communication with the future and the past is possible.

In a recent book called Time--The Familiar Stranger, J.T. Fraser (1987) writes:

> For a photon traveling at the speed of light, the passage of time has no reality. In the "life" of a photon, all events happen at once and all distances shrink to zero.

3. Experimental Results Supporting Quantum Brain/Mind/Consciousness

Several published research studies support with empirical data the proposed quantum consciousness model in this paper. In 1993, in the University of Mexico, neurophysiologist Jacobo Grin-berg-Zylberbaum conducted experiments involving the brain activity of paired students. Two people meditated together with the intention of direct (signal-less, nonlocal) communication. After twenty minutes, they were separated (while still continuing their unifying intention), placed in individual Faraday cages (electromagnetically impervious chambers), and each brain was wired up to an electroencephalogram (EEG) machine. One subject was shown a series of light flashes producing in his or her brain an electrical activity that was recorded in the EEG machine, producing an "evoked potential" extracted by a computer from the brain noise. Surprisingly, the same evoked potential was found to appear in the other subject's brain, and

Scientific GOD Journal | August 2018 | Volume 9 | Issue 6 | pp. 445-466
Valverde, R., *Quantum Theory, Consciousness, God & the Theology of the Urantia Book*

viewable on the EEG of this subject (again minus brain noise). This is called a "transferred potential," but is similar to the evoked potential in phase and strength (Grinberg-Zylberbaum et al. 1987). This experimented supported the concept that consciousness is non-local.

Wackermann, et. al (2003) conducted an experiment where six channels electroencephalogram (EEG) were recorded simultaneously from pairs of separated human subjects in two acoustically and electromagnetically shielded rooms. The results indicate that correlations between brain activities of two separated subjects may occur, although no biophysical mechanism is known. This also supporting the non-local property of human consciousness.

Persinger et. al (2010) performed an experiment with magnetic stimulations of the brain in order to recreated non-local correlations. The experiment concluded that the human brain is the focus of all human experiences. The substantial microstructural and neuroelectrical differences between the two cerebral hemispheres predicts two major classes of mystical experiences which involve the sensed presence and the out-of-body experience. Direct cerebral electrical stimulation during the 20th century evoked these experiences.

Persinger et. al (2003) conducted an experiment with four pairs of adult siblings served once as either the stimulus or the response person in two sessions separated by one week. While the brain of the stimulus person, who was seated in a closed chamber, was exposed successively to six different complex magnetic fields for 5 min. each quantitative monopolar electroencephalographic measurements over the frontal, temporal, parietal, and occipital lobes were collected by computer for the response person who was seated in another room. The results suggest that an appropriate altered state of one brain can effect specific predictable frequencies of the electroencephalographic activity of another distant brain which is genetically related also supporting the non-local property of human consciousness.

Early experiments conducted that prove that consciousness is responsible for the collapse of the wave function were criticized mainly because the subjective component that require an individual to state when he or she observes the wave function. Some scientists have argued that is not human consciousness that collapses the wave function but the environment. The 'subjective reduction' interpretation of measurement in quantum physics proposes that the collapse of the wave-packet, associated with measurement, is due to the consciousness of human observers. A refined conceptual replication of an earlier experiment, designed and carried out to test this interpretation in the 1970s, is reported by Bierman (2003). Two improvements are introduced. First, the delay between pre-observation and final observation of the same quantum event is increased from a few microseconds in the original experiment to one second in this replication. Second, rather than using the final observers' verbal response as the dependent variable, his early brain responses as measured by EEG are used. The results confirm the collapse of the wave function but this time not confirmed by verbal confirmation but by EEG measurements in order to avoid the argument of bias and environment as responsible for this phenomenon.

Germine (1998) performed a study, where random and uncertain stimuli are generated by radioactive decay and recorded on two separate disks. These data are observed by a human subject, whereby the data are collapsed in the consciousness of that subject. The same data are later observed by a second subject. It is proposed that there is a cognitive process that occurs when the wavefunction is collapsed, which is manifested in recordings of electrical potential. These electrical-potential changes will occur in the first subject, who is collapsing the unobserved and therefore uncertain data, but not in the second, who is observing collapses and therefore certain data. The two subjects will alternately observe the two data conditions, and a record of the brain-potential difference between the two conditions for each subject will be determined. Any statistical differences observed when all other variables are controlled will relate to brain processes associated with collapse of the wavefunction. Such results supported the hypothesis that the collapse of the wavefunction is a universal mental process.

Another evidence of the non locality of quantum consciousness is proposed by John Lorber (1981) that specialized in children with hydrocephalus, or water on the brain. Children with this condition have an abnormal amount of cerebral spinal fluid accumulation in the cavities inside their brain compressing brain tissue that usually leads to mental retardation seizures, paralysis and blindness and if not treated to death. Lorber describes dozens of children and some adults with severe hydrocephalus but live normal lives. Indeed, in a sample of children with their cerebral space filled with ninety-five percent of spinal fluid in their skull leaving virtually no room for any brain tissue, half of them had a higher IQ than one hundred and thirty.

Penrose and Hameroff (2011) have argued that that the human brain is a quantum computer and that quantum computations occur in the brain materially and literally. More important, it is exactly this kind of quantum computations in the brain that leads to the mind in general and consciousness in particular. Much effort has been taken to pinpoint how quantum computations are carried out neurophysically, for example, through entangled microtubules in neurons connected and synchronized by gap junctions. When entanglement collapses by "orchestrated objective reduction," a fundamental effect of quantum gravity, consciousness arises. Recently, this Orch OR state reduction is linked to the gamma band EEG signal in the brain ($\sim$40 Hz), suggesting a $\sim$25-ms rhythm of conscious progression.

Hitchcock (2003) a quantum computing model of the brain called T-computer that is in charge of linearizing events in order to create time. T-computers are essential to our maps of reality. They are used to create ordered sets of time labeled observed events or whose 'linear' or non-linear causal time ordering may be the location of the infostates representing the events in memory and their contents. An infostate of a system is the set of configuration observables for that system along with the information content usually expressed as the wavefunction for the system. Information originates in quantum system and is processed as quantum or classical states of the neural networks of our brains. The model supports the idea that time is just a sequence of events created by the brain from the quantum reality.

4. Urantia book

The Urantia Book (1996) is a spiritual and philosophical book that originated in Chicago
sometime between 1924 and 1955. The authors introduce the word "Urantia" as the name of the
planet Earth and state that their intent is to "present enlarged concepts and advanced truth". The
book aims to unite religion, science and philosophy, and its enormous amount of material about
science is unique among literature. Among other topics, the book discusses the origin and
meaning of life, humankind's place in the universe, the relationship between God and people, and
the life of Jesus.

The Urantia Foundation, a U.S.-based non-profit group, first published The Urantia Book in
1955. The book and its publishers do not name a human author. Instead, it is written as if directly
presented by numerous celestial beings appointed to the task of providing an "epochal" religious
revelation. As early as 1911, William S. Sadler and his wife Lena Sadler, physicians in Chicago
and well known in the community, are said to have been approached by a neighbor who was
concerned because she would occasionally find her husband in a deep sleep and breathing
abnormally (Mullins & Sprunger 2000).

The Sadlers came to observe the episodes, and over time, the individual produced verbal
communications that claimed to be from "student visitor" spiritual beings. This changed
sometime in early 1925 with a "voluminous handwritten document," which from then on became
the regular method of purported communication. The individual was never identified publicly but
has been described as "a hard-boiled business man, member of the board of trade and stock
exchange" (Mullins & Sprunger 2000).

The Sadlers were both respected physicians, and William Sadler was a debunker of paranormal
claims, who is portrayed as not believing in the supernatural. In 1929, he published a book called
The Mind at Mischief, in which he explained the fraudulent methods of mediums and how
self-deception leads to psychic claims (Mullins & Sprunger 2000).

In 1923, a group of Sadler's friends, former patients, and colleagues began meeting for Sunday
philosophical and religious discussions, but became interested in the strange communications
when Sadler mentioned the case at their fourth meeting and read samples at their request. Shortly
afterwards, a communication reportedly was received about which this group would be allowed
to devise questions and that answers would be given by celestial beings through the "contact
personality". Sadler presented this development to the group, and they generated hundreds of
questions without full seriousness, but their claim is that it resulted in the appearance of answers
in the form of fully written papers. The Sadlers and others involved, now all deceased, claimed
that the papers of the book were physically materialized from 1925 until 1935 in a way that was
not understood even by them, with the first two parts being completed in 1934 and the third and
fourth in 1935. The last Forum gathering was in 1942 (Mullins & Sprunger 2000).

After the last of Part IV was obtained in 1935, an additional period of time supposedly took place
where requests for clarifications resulted in revisions. Sadler and his son William (Bill) Sadler, Jr

Scientific GOD Journal | August 2018 | Volume 9 | Issue 6 | pp. 445-466
Valverde, R., *Quantum Theory, Consciousness, God & the Theology of the Urantia Book*

at one point wrote a draft introduction and were told that they could not add their introduction. The Foreword was then "received". The communications purportedly continued for another two decades while members of the Forum studied the book in depth, and according to Sadler and others, permission to publish it was given to them in 1955 (Mullins & Sprunger 2000).

The Urantia Book is claimed to be, a presentation of truth to us, about the creator and about creation. It greatly expands our view and understanding of the creator and the cosmos, and with this bigger picture, science, religion, and history, and other areas of human knowledge become integrated. We are not alone in the universe, quite the contrary. The Urantia Book was written by love - respecting, civilized inhabitants of the universe. It was written by a revelatory committee, through a process involving a contact human, for the betterment of our planet. The identity of the contact human is not known, and not considered important. Urantia is the name of our planet (Mullins & Sprunger 2000).

The Urantia Book revelation is not small; the edition quoted has 2,097 pages of fine print. For most of us, it is not a quick study or easy reading. The Urantia Book is valuable, for it reveals a much larger perspective than was previously known on Earth regarding God, the universe's inhabitants, and the cosmos in which we live. The revelations from the Urantia Book are presented in four parts. Part 1, The Central and Superuniverses, is about God, God's relationship to creation, God's relationship to individuals, and the structure and inhabitants of the greater cosmos. Part 2, The Local Universe, is about our part of the cosmos. It presents topics including creation, evolution, administration, and the various inhabitants of our local universe. Part 3, The History of Urantia, includes information about the origin of our planet, and about its physical, biological, and social evolution. Part 4, The Life and Teachings of Jesus, is self - explanatory (Mullins & Sprunger 2000).

The Urantia Book is approximately 2,000 pages long, and consists of a body of 196 "papers" divided in four parts, and an introductory forward:

- Part I, titled "The Central and Superuniverses", addresses what the authors consider the highest levels of creation, including the eternal and infinite "Universal Father", his Trinity associates, and the "Isle of Paradise".

- Part II, "The Local Universe", describes the origin, administration, and personalities of the local universe of "Nebadon", the part of the cosmos where Earth resides. It presents narratives on the inhabitants of local universes and their work as it is coordinated with a scheme of spiritual ascension and progression of different orders of beings, including humans, angels, and others.

- Part III, "The History of Urantia", compiles a broad history of the Earth, presenting a purported explanation of the origin, evolution, and destiny of the world and its inhabitants. Topics include Adam and Eve, Melchizedek, essays on the concept of the Thought Adjuster, "Religion in Human Experience", and "Personality Survival".

- Part IV, "The Life and Teachings of Jesus", is the largest part at 775 pages, and is often

42

Scientific GOD Journal | August 2018 | Volume 9 | Issue 6 | pp. 445-466
Valverde, R., *Quantum Theory, Consciousness, God & the Theology of the Urantia Book*

noted as the most accessible and most impressive, narrating a detailed biography of Jesus that includes his childhood, teenage years, family life, and public ministry, as well as the events that led to his crucifixion, death, and resurrection. Its papers continue about appearances after he rose, Pentecost and, finally, "The Faith of Jesus".

5. Proposed Quantum Consciousness Model

The proposed quantum consciousness model has seven statements that are based on the literature review and experimental results discussed in previous sections. The seven proposed statements are:

1. What consciousness is able to perceive with its five senses is not reality. Quantum physics has shown that space and time are illusions of perception. Our body cannot really be a reality if it does not occupy most of the space it seems to occupy, quantum physics revealed that the shape of the interior of an atom is almost entirely empty space and that matter is made of concentrated vibrating energy. Time is also an illusion and it represents a sequence of linear events that the brain generates based on perceived energy around every 25 milliseconds.

2. The model proposes that consciousness is non-local and can work independently of the physical brain. Nonlocality or "action at a distance" is the nature of consciousness. Human Consciousness is non-spatial and non-temporal and not in the brain but in prespacetime. Consciousness is multidimensional, it can exist outside the three-dimensional reality.

3. The model explains that we live in a collective consciousness that connects all the consciousnesses of the universe to the supreme consciousness.

4. Consciousness is likely play important roles in quantum effects such as in the wave function collapse, this is the foundation of the reality that we perceive.

5. Conscious intentions likely have physical effects on matter at distance due to the entanglement quantum effect.

6. Materialistic theories for the explanation of consciousness are likely invalid (Neuroscience).

7. Brain is a computer processor and interface between human Consciousness and the external world.

6. Consciousness connection to God, Urantia Book and Quantum Theory

In the past there has seemed to be a deep conflict between science and religion over which it was difficult to pass. Science has been able to explain much in religion that was formerly blind belief, and religion can give vitality to cold scientific facts and make them vibrate with life.

Quantum physics is perhaps a possible answer to the scientific explanation of God's living within our consciousness. Quantum physics explains that the universe is made of quantum particles that are the cells of the universe and vibrating particles make different forms of energy and matter. Quantum physics explains that at the quantum level, particles that come from the same source are entangled regardless of space and time (Horodecki et. al 2009). This means that two entangled particles can affect and communicate with each other instantaneously regardless of space between them. The Urantia book (1996), explains that souls are created from a source of light from a central universe where the universal mind resides.

Jesus said according to the Gospel of St Thomas, "If your leaders say to you, 'Look, the (Father's) kingdom is in the sky,' then the birds of the sky will precede you. If they say to you, 'It is in the sea,' then the fish will precede you. Rather, the (Father's) kingdom is within you and it is outside you. When you know yourselves, then you will be known, and you will understand that you are children of the living Father. But if you do not know yourselves, then you live in poverty, and you are the poverty."

It means that the only place that we can really find God is within. A scientific explanation to the Christian concept that God lives within is us could be explained with quantum entanglement, if our quantum particles are unified with the Universal mind that resides in a central universe according to the Urantia book, this Universal consciousness can be connected to us regardless of space and be able to understand our feelings and emotions through quantum particle vibrations. If each human vibrates at a given frequency, God or Universal mind can identify the consciousness that is sending a particular vibration. There is an infinite number of frequencies that can be assigned to each human consciousness. So, the idea that God live within us can be explained with science and the idea that love is vibration can help us to understand that God's love really lives in us. God can really live through us and experience our lives. God is willing to reveal his nature to those that are willing to look within and communicate to him through the divine consciousness.

7. Quantum Consciousness Model & the Urantia Book

In this section, portions of the Urantia book that support the proposed quantum consciousness model are presented with a brief explanation on how each portion supports the model. Table 1

44

presents the principle(s) supported by each Urantia book reference with the corresponding explanation.

Table 1. Urantia book and consciousness model

Quantum Consciousness model principle(s)	Urantia book reference	Quote from the Urantia book that supports quantum consciousness model principle	Explanation about how the Urantia book supports the quantum
1	12:5.1	... Time comes by virtue of motion and because mind is inherently aware of sequentiality.	Time is an illusion and it represents a sequence of linear events that the brain generates from quantum energy.
1	12:5.5	Relationships to time do not exist without motion in space, but consciousness of time does. Sequentiality can consciousize time even in the absence of motion. Man's mind is less time-bound than space-bound because of the inherent nature of mind.	Time is an illusion and it represents a sequence of linear events that the brain generates from quantum energy.
1	12:5.7	There are three different levels of time cognizance: 1. Mind-perceived time — consciousness of sequence, motion, and a sense of duration.	Time is an illusion and it represents a sequence of linear events that the brain generates from quantum energy.
2	12:8.7	.........the phenomenon of mind, is the exclusive domain of the Conjoint Actor, who thus becomes the partner of the spiritual mind, the essence of the morontia mind, and the substance of the material mind of the evolutionary creatures of time.	The Conjoint Actor personalizes as an unlimited spirituality, co-ordinated with absolute mind, and with prerogatives of energy manipulation. The mortal intellect, as such, has perished, has ceased to exist as a focalized universe entity apart from the undifferentiated mind circuits of the Creative

			Spirit. But the meanings and values of the mortal mind have not perished. Certain phases of mind are continued in the surviving soul. Consciousness is multidimensional, it can exist outside the three-dimensional reality.
1, 4	12:8.10	Matter. Organized energy which is subject to linear gravity except as it is modified by motion and conditioned by mind.	The book confirms that matter is nothing more than concentrated energy that is linked to consciousness. Matter is conditioned by mind.
6	12:8.11	Mind. Organized consciousness which is not wholly subject to material gravity, and which becomes truly liberated when modified by spirit.	Materialistic theories for the explanation of consciousness are likely invalid according to this statement. True consciousness has no material origin and it is not subject to the physical laws of gravity.
6	12:8.14	On Paradise the three energies, physical, mindal, and spiritual, are co-ordinate. In the evolutionary cosmos energy-matter is dominant except in personality, where spirit, through the mediation of mind, is striving for the mastery.	The true essence of consciousness is not material.
4	12:8.15	In cosmic evolution matter becomes a philosophic shadow cast by mind in the presence of spirit luminosity of divine enlightenment, but this does not invalidate the reality of matter-energy. Mind, matter, and spirit are equally real, but they are	Matter is the product of consciousness, real but not of equal value in the evolution of spirit.

		not of equal value to personality in the attainment of divinity.	
2,3 4, 6	12:8.16	The brighter the shining of the spiritualized personality (the Father in the universe, the fragment of potential spirit personality in the individual creature), the greater the shadow cast by the intervening mind upon its material investment. In time, man's body is just as real as mind or spirit, but in death, both mind (identity) and spirit survive while the body does not.	Consciousness is non local and can work independently of the physical brain as it survives mortal death. Consciousness is connected to the supreme consciousness due to the fragment that indwell in the individual True consciousness is non material as it does not die with mortal death. Matter is a creation of the mind.
1	42:0.1	The foundation of the universe is material in the sense that energy is the basis of all existence, and pure energy is controlled by the Universal Father.	Matter is made of concentrated vibrating energy.
4	42:2.5	Space potency is a prereality; it is the domain of the Unqualified Absolute and is responsive only to the personal grasp of the Universal Father,	Space potency is the source of energy for the creation of reality (prereality). All material reality is created from this source and molded by consciousness.
1	42:4.14	The quantity of energy taken in or given out when electronic or other positions are shifted is always a " quantum " or some multiple thereof, but the vibratory or wavelike behavior of such units of energy is wholly determined by the dimensions of the material structures concerned.	Matter is made of concentrated vibrating energy
2	42:10.7	Paradise mind is beyond human understanding; it is existential,	Human Consciousness is non-spatial and

Scientific GOD Journal | August 2018 | Volume 9 | Issue 6 | pp. 445-466
Valverde, R., *Quantum Theory, Consciousness, God & the Theology of the Urantia Book*

			nonspatial, and nontemporal.	non-temporal and not in the brain but in prespacetime
4,5	42:11.1		In the evaluation and recognition of mind it should be remembered that the universe is neither mechanical nor magical; it is a creation of mind and a mechanism of law.	Consciousness is likely play important roles in quantum effects such as in the wave function collapse, this is the foundation of the reality that we perceive. Conscious intentions likely have physical effects on matter at distance due to the entanglement quantum effect.
7	42:12.12		On a material world you think of a body as having a spirit, but we regard the spirit as having a body. The material eyes are truly the windows of the spirit-born soul. The spirit is the architect, the mind is the builder, the body is the material building.	Brain is a computer processor and interface between human Consciousness and the external world. The brain are the eyes of consciousness.
4,5	42:12.14		The spirit is the creative reality; the physical counterpart is the time-space reflection of the spirit reality, the physical repercussion of the creative action of spirit-mind.	Consciousness is likely play important roles in quantum effects such as in the wave function collapse, this is the foundation of the reality that we perceive. Conscious intentions likely have physical effects on matter at distance due to the entanglement quantum effect.
3	112:1.2		Position status. Personality functions equally efficiently in the local universe, in the superuniverse,	Consciousness is multidimensional, it can exist outside the

48

		and in the central universe.	three-dimensional reality.
3	112:1.17	.....individual members are not connected with each other except in relation to the whole and through the individuality of the whole.	The model explains that we live in a collective consciousness that connects all the consciousnesses of the universe to the supreme consciousness.
4	130:4.1	.........Jesus gave qualified approval of some of the Greek teachings which had to do with the theory that the material things of the world are shadowy reflections of invisible but more substantial spiritual realities, he sought to lay a more trustworthy foundation for the lad's thinking; so he began a long dissertation concerning the nature of reality in the universe.	Consciousness is likely play important roles in quantum effects such as in the wave function collapse, this is the foundation of the reality that we perceive.
6	130:4.4	A one-eyed person can never hope to visualize depth of perspective. Neither can single-eyed material scientists nor single-eyed spiritual mystics and allegorists correctly visualize and adequately comprehend the true depths of universe reality.	Materialistic theories for the explanation of consciousness are likely invalid (Neuroscience). Consciousness understating requires a spiritual and materialistic views.
7	130:4.10	Knowledge is the sphere of the material or fact-discerning mind. Truth is the domain of the spiritually endowed intellect that is conscious of knowing God. Knowledge is demonstrable; truth is experienced. Knowledge is a possession of the mind; truth an experience of the soul, the progressing self. Knowledge is a function of the nonspiritual level;	Brain is a computer processor and interface between human Consciousness. and the external world. Fact is the domain of the brain but the truth is the domain of consciousness.

		truth is a phase of the mind-spirit level of the universes. The eye of the material mind perceives a world of factual knowledge; the eye of the spiritualized intellect discerns a world of true values. These two views, synchronized and harmonized, reveal the world of reality, wherein wisdom interprets the phenomena of the universe in terms of progressive personal experience.	
1	130:7.4	Time is the stream of flowing temporal events perceived by creature consciousness. Time is a name given to the succession-arrangement whereby events are recognized and segregated.	Time is also an illusion and it represents a sequence of linear events that the brain generates based on perceived energy around every 25 milliseconds.
1	130:7.5	Animals do not sense time as does man, and even to man, because of his sectional and circumscribed view, time appears as a succession of events; but as man ascends, as he progresses inward, the enlarging view of this event procession is such that it is discerned more and more in its wholeness. That which formerly appeared as a succession of events then will be viewed as a whole and perfectly related cycle; in this way will circular simultaneity increasingly displace the onetime consciousness of the linear sequence of events.	Time is also an illusion and it represents a sequence of linear events that the brain generates based on perceived energy around every 25 milliseconds. There is no past or future but only a constant present.
1	130:7.6	There are seven different conceptions of space as it is conditioned by time. Space is measured by time, not time by	What consciousness is able to perceive with its five senses is not reality. Quantum physics has

		space. The confusion of the scientist grows out of failure to recognize the reality of space. Space is not merely an intellectual concept of the variation in relatedness of universe objects. Space is not empty, and the only thing man knows which can even partially transcend space is mind. Mind can function independently of the concept of the space-relatedness of material objects. Space is relatively and comparatively finite to all beings of creature status.	shown that space and time are illusions of perception.	
2	130:7.8	The time-space concept of a mind of material origin is destined to undergo successive enlargements as the conscious and conceiving personality ascends the levels of the universes. When man attains the mind intervening between the material and the spiritual planes of existence, his ideas of time-space will be enormously expanded both as to quality of perception and quantity of experience. ....the time-space concept will increasingly approximate the timeless and spaceless concepts of the Absolutes.	The model proposes that consciousness is non local and can work independently of the physical brain.	
1	118:1.9	On the levels of the infinite and the absolute the moment of the present contains all of the past as well as all of the future. I AM signifies also I WAS and I WILL BE. And this represents our best concept of eternity and the eternal.	Time is also an illusion and it represents a sequence of linear events that the brain generates based on perceived energy around every 25 milliseconds. There is no future or past but just a constant present.	
1	118:3.1	Only by ubiquity could Deity unify	What consciousness is	

		time-space manifestations to the finite conception, for time is a succession of instants while space is a system of associated points. You do, after all, perceive time by analysis and space by synthesis. You co-ordinate and associate these two dissimilar conceptions by the integrating insight of personality. Of all the animal world only man possesses this time-space perceptibility. To an animal, motion has a meaning, but motion exhibits value only to a creature of personality status.	able to perceive with its five senses is not reality. Quantum physics has shown that space and time are illusions of perception.
1	118:3.5	Space comes the nearest of all nonabsolute things to being absolute. Space is apparently absolutely ultimate. The real difficulty we have in understanding space on the material level is due to the fact that, while material bodies exist in space, space also exists in these same material bodies. While there is much about space that is absolute, that does not mean that space is absolute.	What consciousness is able to perceive with its five senses is not reality. Quantum physics has shown that space and time are illusions of perception. Our body cannot really be a reality if it does not occupy most of the space it seems to occupy, quantum physics revealed that the shape of the interior of an atom is almost entirely empty space and that matter is made of concentrated vibrating energy.
1	118:3.6	It may help to an understanding of space relationships if you would conjecture that, relatively speaking, space is after all a property of all material bodies. Hence, when a body moves through space, it also takes all its properties with it, even the space which is in and of such a	What consciousness is able to perceive with its five senses is not reality. Quantum physics has shown that space and time are illusions of perception. Our body cannot really be a reality if it does not

		moving body.	occupy most of the space it seems to occupy, quantum physics revealed that the shape of the interior of an atom is almost entirely empty space....
1	118:3.7	All patterns of reality occupy space on the material levels, but spirit patterns only exist in relation to space; they do not occupy or displace space, neither do they contain it.	What consciousness is able to perceive with its five senses is not reality. Quantum physics has shown that space and time are illusions of perception. Our body cannot really be a reality if it does not occupy most of the space it seems to occupy, quantum physics revealed that the shape of the interior of an atom is almost entirely empty space and that matter is made of concentrated vibrating energy.
6, 7	118:8.2	Mortal man is a machine, a living mechanism; his roots are truly in the physical world of energy. Many human reactions are mechanical in nature; much of life is machinelike. But man, a mechanism, is much more than a machine; he is mind endowed and spirit indwelt; and though he can never throughout his material life escape the chemical and electrical mechanics of his existence, he can increasingly learn how to subordinate this physical-life machine to the directive wisdom of experience by the process of consecrating the	Materialistic theories for the explanation of consciousness are likely invalid (Neuroscience). Brain is a computer processor and interface between human Consciousness and the external world.

		human mind to the execution of the spiritual urges of the indwelling Thought Adjuster.	
3	118:9.4	The grand universe is mechanism as well as organism, mechanical and living—a living mechanism activated by a Supreme Mind, co-ordinating with a Supreme Spirit, and finding expression on maximum levels of power and personality unification as the Supreme Being. But to deny the mechanism of the finite creation is to deny fact and to disregard reality.	The model explains that we live in a collective consciousness that connects all the consciousnesses of the universe to the supreme consciousness.
6	118:10.13	.....As long as men measure only by the yardstick of the things of a physical nature, they can never hope to find unity in time and space.	Materialistic theories for the explanation of consciousness are likely invalid (Neuroscience).
4	16:9.1	....personal creature possesses innate recognition-realization of energy reality, mind reality, and spirit reality. ....Aside from these three inalienables of human consciousness, all human experience is really subjective except that intuitive realization of validity attaches to the *unification* of these three universe reality responses of cosmic recognition.	Consciousness is likely play important roles in quantum effects such as in the wave function collapse, this is the foundation of the reality that we perceive.
2	16:9.3	If mortal man fails to survive natural death, the real spiritual values of his human experience survive as a part of the continuing experience of the Thought Adjuster.	The model proposes that consciousness is non local and can work independently of the physical brain.

8. Conclusions

In this article, a quantum consciousness model with seven principles is proposed and supported with literature review and experimental results from published literature. The Urantia book is introduced as a revelation that aims to unite religion, science and philosophy. The idea that Quantum physics is a possible answer to the scientific explanation of God's living within our consciousness was introduced and supported with the Urantia book concept tht God is a source of energy residing in the central universe. The Urantia book reveals the nature of human consciousness and supports with its theology the proposed quantum consciousness model. The article introduces the Urantia book as a source of knowledge that has the intention to reconciliate religion paradigms with consciousness studies. Future research would be focused in expanding the proposed quantum consciousness model with the help of the Urantia book and using this source of knowledge to support a more scientific view of God that helps to reconciliate science and religion.

References

Beynam, Laurence M. (1978) "The Emergent Paradigm in Science," Revision, Spring.

Bierman, J. B. (2003). Does consciousness collapse the wave-packet? Mind & Matter; 1(1): 45-77

Bohm, D. (1980). Wholeness and the Implicate Order. London: Routledge and Kegan Paul.

Davies, P. (1988). The Cosmic Blueprint. New York: Simon and Schuster,.

Fraser, J.T. (1987). Time, the familiar stranger. Univ of Massachusetts Press.

Germine, M (1998). Experimental Model for Collapse of the Wavefunction. Dynamical Psychology.

Greyson, B. & Stevenson, I (1980). The phenomenology of near-death experiences. The American journal of psychiatry.

Griffin, David R. (Editor) (1986). Physics and the Ultimate Significance of Time. Albany: State University of New York Press.

Grinberg-Zylberbaum, J. & Ramos, J. (1987), Patterns of interhemispheric correlation during human communication. International Journal of Neuroscience; 36: 41–53.

Hameroff S. (1998). Quantum computation in brain microtubules? The Penrose-Hameroff Orch OR'model of consciousness. Philosophical Transactions-Royal Society of London Series A Mathematical Physical and Engineering Sciences, 25:1869-95.

Hitchcock SM (2003). T-computers and the Origins of Time in the Brain. NeuroQuantology. Jan 1;1(4).

Horodecki, R., Horodecki, P., Horodecki, M., & Horodecki, K. (2009). Quantum entanglement. Reviews of modern physics, 81(2), 865.

Hu H, Wu M (2010). Current landscape and future direction of theoretical & experimental quantum brain/mind/consciousness research. Journal of Consciousness Exploration & Research. 9;1(8).

Hu H, Wu M (2013). The Relationship between Human Consciousness & Universal Consciousness. Scientific GOD Journal. 28;4(3).

Josephson, B. D. (1962). Possible new effects in superconductive tunnelling. Physics letters, 1(7), 251-253.

Lorber, J. (1981). Is your brain really necessary?. Nursing mirror, 152(18), 29-30.

Scientific GOD Journal | August 2018 | Volume 9 | Issue 6 | pp. 445-466
Valverde, R., *Quantum Theory, Consciousness, God & the Theology of the Urantia Book*

Marshall, I. and Zohar, D (1997). Who's afraid of Schrödinger's cat. New York: Quill/William Morrow.

Mullins, L. and Sprunger, M.J (2000). A History of the URANTIA Papers (p. 5). Boulder, CO: Penumbra Press.

Penrose, Roger (1994). Shadows of the Mind. Vol. 4. Oxford: Oxford University Press.

Penrose, R., & Hameroff, S. (2011). Consciousness in the universe: Neuroscience, quantum space-time geometry and Orch OR theory. Journal of Cosmology, 14, 1-17.

Persinger, M.A., Koren, S.A. & Tsang, E.W., (2003). Enhanced power within a specific band of theta activity in one person while another receives circumcerebral pulsed magnetic fields: a mechanism for cognitive influence at a distance?. Perceptual and Motor Skills, 97(3), pp.877-894.

Persinger, M.A., Saroka, K.S., Koren, S.A. and St-Pierre, L.S., (2010). The electromagnetic induction of mystical and altered states within the laboratory. Journal of Consciousness Exploration & Research, 1(7), pp.808-830

Russell, R.J., Murphy, N. and Isham, C.J. (1993), Quantum cosmology and the laws of nature: scientific perspectives on divine action.

The Urantia Book (1994). Uversa Press, Chicago.

Valverde, R (2015a), Possible Role of Quantum Physics in Transpersonal & Metaphysical Psychology. Journal of Consciousness Exploration & Research. 7(4): 303-309.

Valverde, R. (2015b). Channeling as an Altered State of Consciousness in Transpersonal Psychology Therapy. Journal of Consciousness Exploration & Research, 6(7).

Valverde, R. (2016). A Quantum Biofeedback and Neurotechnology Cybertherapy System for the Support of Transpersonal Psychotherapy. NeuroQuantology, 14(4).

Wackermann, J. (2003), Seiter, C., Keibel, H. and Walach, H. Correlations between brain electrical activities of two spatially separated human subjects. NeuroScience letters, 336(1), pp.60-64.

Wolf, F. A. (1984). Star Wave. New York: Macmillan, 1984.

Made in the USA
Coppell, TX
09 September 2021